The Life *and* Legacy *of*

Donald Goines

LOW ROAD

The Life *and* Legacy *of*

Donald Goines

Eddie B. Allen, Jr.

LOW ROAD

St. Martin's Press 📖 New York

For Dad, who taught me to believe

www.stmartins.com

ISBN 0-312-29124-8

First Edition: October 2004

Contents

Acknowledgments

All praises are due to the One divine and unparalleled Creator for the opportunity to take part in documenting the life discussed in these pages.

Low Road: The Life and Legacy of Donald Goines is the result of a community effort that could not have been sustained to completion without prayers, support, time, encouragement, and other valuable resources provided by the following: Eddie B. Allen, Sr., and Linell Allen; Charles Glover; my agent and the wonderful ambassador of kwan, Susan Raihofer, who played Mick to my humble Rocky; Joan Coney and Marie Richardson; Monique Patterson and St. Martin's Press, who took the chance; DMX and Brandon Himmel; attorneys Larry Pepper and Barbara Cohen; Paul Lee/Best Efforts, Inc.; Curtis Jamaal Allen; Sam Greenlee; Imelda Hunt/New Works Writers Series; Fred Girard; Dr. Kenneth Cole; John Hollowell; Janet and Bill Mitchum; Maurice Armstrong; Joe Williams; Lisa Montez; my older, wiser sister, Robyn, and the entire Ussery clan; Craig Ciccone; Wil Segars; Ralph Watts; Tim Pharaoh Muhammad; Lisa B. Lee; Roman Godzak; C. Liegh

McInnis; Bentley Morriss; Neal Colgrass; Susan Strunk; William Shackleford; Brenda V. Peek; LaShaun Moore; Janerio Morgan; Shondra Tipler; Peter Goldman; Alisa Giddens; Eric Levin; Racquel Ward; Raymond Stevens; Walter Williamson; Marie Teasley; Maisha Maurant; Erik Perry/Kaboodlz Entertainment; Gil Robertson; Kim Trent; Terrence and Kendra Collier; Phyllis Pollack; Denise Crittendon; Sandra Combs-Birdiett; Steven G. Fullwood; Sonya Vann; Jack Lessenberry; Dwight Cunningham; Rev. Charles "Slim" Lake and my friends at God's Church of the Streets; Lynda Crist; William Cooper, Jr.; Ruth Seymour; Ozzie Bruno; Gary Pomerantz; Betty Dooley; Samuel "Rickey" Rowe; Leri Ulmer; Jim Lesar; Liberty R. O. Daniels; Nicholas Parham; Tumika Patrice Cain; Tonya and Brandi Neal; U.S. Navy Master Diver (Ret.) Michael Washington; Bill Thomas; Charles Muhammad and the Self Expression Teen Theater board, staff, and students; Jon Richardson; Jelani Jebari; Christopher Woodard; Rochelle Riley-Wilson; James McCarter, Keith Dye, Toni Smith, Vic Doucette, and Dennis Shea; James and Karla Aren; Ben and Gloria Crain; "Cousin" Ray Allen; Larry Davis; Jacqueline Hardy; Stewart Walker; Mansour Bey; Jerry Jones; Alicia Densemo; Dayjanae Mathews; Marcel Riddick; Toya Hankins; Charlie and Karen Thomas; Margaret and Donna Stevenson; Tricia McCaffrey; John Robinson Block and my friends from The Blade in Toledo; lastly, the most patient and helpful staffs of the Detroit Public Library's Burton Historical Collection and the Family History Center in Bloomfield Hills.

All praises, all praises, and all praises.

Foreword

The year 2004 marked the thirtieth anniversary of Donald Goines's death. It also marked the year that I produced my first film, *Never Die Alone*, based on the thirty-year-old Goines book. I've read every Donald Goines novel; so as soon as I heard that there was an opportunity for one of them to be turned into a movie, I jumped at the chance.

I was locked up when I first heard of him, when I first read his books. Here were a set of novels that didn't always have a happy ending. He wrote about a lot of things that I could relate to. A lot of the characters I knew. King David's story of living a grimy life, going through personal pain, and gaining a conscience is very relevant to the plight of the black man today. I didn't like the character. He's a bastard, and I'm not a grimy person—I've come through that stage—but I knew enough about him to try to make him real. I don't think King David is as amped as I am, and I talk kind of fast, so I had to slow it down. Like an old man talkin' shit to the young players.

For all the terrible things he's done, he doesn't see himself as beyond redemption. But reality hits, and despite the fact that he's coming to terms with some of the wrongs that he's committed, he still gets what he deserves. The message is, "You do dirt; you get dirt."

This is a theme with many of the Goines characters. No matter what crisis or trouble pushed them into crime, they get it in the end. I think Donald Goines understood this about life and wanted us to understand it: Everything we do has a price.

His writing has already inspired me to produce another film. We're going to do *Daddy Cool*. I don't know if I'll play Daddy Cool. I'm not going to star in every one of my movies. But what I will bring to the film industry is the same thing I brought to the record industry when I came into it—the same thing Donald Goines brought to his books—realism. Uncompromised, unconditional "dog love." Not love for *everybody,* but we'll have a clique, we'll be tight, and we'll bring real, official shit to the table. No fake, animated representations. The truth in undeniable. Show somebody the truth, and it can't be ignored. This is what Donald Goines did. Even though it's presented as fiction, truth can be taken from every book.

And even in death, he's still real.

—DMX
(a.k.a. "King David," of the Fox Searchlight motion picture
Never Die Alone)
March 2004

Preface

I can clearly remember the vivid image of the brown-skinned man with the outstretched arm that adorned the paperback cover of my cousin's book. His sleeve was rolled into a bunch as he prepared to inject himself with a syringe. Above the illustration was the word *Dopefiend*. I was probably about nine or ten at the time. My cousin was perhaps sixteen or seventeen.

She read the book intently as we traveled down the highway, my dad at the wheel and Ma riding shotgun. We were on our way to some summer destination or another, as was my family's custom when school let out and the days became long. My uncle's daughters were frequently recruited to baby-sit me, particularly when adult activities, like a Bid Whist game, were in the plans or when there was the possibility of a visit to Cedar Point or a similar amusement park not far away.

I contented myself in the backseat with Rosa, tilting over head-first onto her shoulder as the steady motion of the vehicle guided me toward sleep. I probably drooled on her arm. It wasn't until maybe ten years later when I once again encountered the book that had so engrossed my cousin. A copy of *Dopefiend* somehow wound up on the shelf of my parents' library. Remembering Rosa's attentiveness, I picked up the book and flipped through its pages.

It didn't take long for me to understand how easily a reader could get lost in the imagery. I found myself taking in the striking descriptions and compelling dialogue as if the characters were acting out scenarios in front of me. Set in the 1970s, *Dopefiend* tells the story of Porky, a morbidly obese loser, who draws his self-esteem and popularity from drug connections. Things run in favor of the social outcast as he participates in the urban dope game. Porky becomes a neighborhood kingpin, with money, respect, and attention from young ladies who would otherwise ignore him. So great is his dominion among the addicts, as a matter of fact, that his female peers perform the most disgusting of sex acts with dogs for his perverse enjoyment, in order to win his grace.

Having decided that I would be a newspaper reporter, specializing in coverage of urban and oppressed people, I appreciated the realism of *Dopefiend*'s account. But I had not learned exactly how real the details of the novel were. They had been taken directly from experiences and observations in the life of Donald Goines. The author had been murdered when I was only two years old.

He and I shared similarities, but had little in common: We were both writers born in Detroit during the month of December. We both had been raised in two-parent, middle-class households. But that's about where it ended.

He was a product of the post–Depression-era city, where men of color still walked a fine line between pride and self-preservation. It was months before his seventh birthday when thirty-six hours of rioting on Belle Isle Park and in neighboring parts of the city left thirty-four dead, twenty-five of whom were black, including a man who had been waiting on a bus at the corner of Mack Avenue and Chene. The eruption, which ended only after state and federal troops arrived to rescue an overwhelmed Detroit Police Department, resulted from a large skirmish on the island, followed by two unfounded rumors: that whites had thrown a black baby off the Belle Isle Bridge and that blacks had raped a white woman.

I, on the other hand, could not recall a Detroit where people of color were the minority. For most of my life the mayor, police chief, and many prominent business owners were black people. Arabs had begun to operate a large number of the gas stations and small grocery stores in the Detroit I knew. White neighbors, teachers, and police officers would not be seen until my parents moved to the northern suburb of Southfield. And even then, if I mumbled when I spoke or failed to make eye contact with any one of them, it was because of my early shyness, not because I had any familiarity whatsoever with racism.

But the biggest difference between us lies not in the eras or environments in which we developed. It was the drugs. I had seen the impact of drugs in my own family. Two loved ones had died as a result of using or selling controlled substances. I have never even smoked a cigarette. I considered, and still consider, drugs to be among the worst enemies our communities have ever faced. Mr. Goines, however, became addicted as a youth and, sadly, lived the majority of his life under the influence of narcotics.

So I had never considered telling a story like his when the friendly young general manager of a small Ohio radio station approached me. I liked Charles Glover. He laughed and smiled a lot, never seeming to take himself too seriously. Mark, a mutual acquaintance, had introduced us during the early months of 1999. I had recently been laid off from a communications job in Detroit and was looking for a freelance opportunity in radio. Mark and I had discussed bringing a public affairs and social commentary show to Charles's station in Toledo, where I'd lived until the previous year.

I wrote several scripts, and Mark helped put music together for our proposed segment. After weeks of discussion about the show's focus and sponsorship possibilities, we had all become comfortable with one another in our working relationship. I can't remember how it came up, but one afternoon as we sat in his office, Charles mentioned that he'd had a "crazy uncle" in Detroit. We chatted a little more until he revealed that he was Mr. Goines's nephew. The memories of my cousin reading in the car and the book I found in my parents' library immediately flashed through my mind.

Charles explained to us that his mother, Marie, was Mr. Goines's older sister. He shared memories of growing up around neighborhoods I recognized, while his grandparents, Aunt Joan and "Uncle Donnie," served as the fabric of his family. He shared how he had approached various writers and literary agents in recent years, hoping to find the person who would recognize the value and significance of a biography about Mr. Goines. There had been one bio, hastily published the same year his uncle died, but Charles said that he and the family regarded it as a poor effort. If I was interested in writing the story, he told me, he would assist by providing not only as many personal recollections as he could produce, but also personal documents, photographs, and other materials that would be helpful in revealing who Mr. Goines was.

To say his offer was unexpected wouldn't accurately capture the feeling. Probably the last thing I imagined I'd hear before returning to Detroit that day was that this easygoing broadcast exec was related to the man responsible for *Dopefiend, Black Girl Lost,* and *Eldorado Red.* I couldn't imagine their seemingly incompatible personas having anything to do with one another. But I guess I processed it all rather quickly.

I had considered writing a biography on another subject prior to our meeting, though under more ordinary circumstances. It moved me that Charles thought enough of my character, not to mention my abilities, that he would trust me to tell his uncle's story. I accepted the invitation and we agreed to get together for as many meetings and exchanges of information as it took for me to create a written account of the Goines legacy. What followed was approximately two years of research.

The work that resulted is largely based on a series of interviews with Charles; his mother, Marie Richardson; his aunt, Joan Coney; and other family members, friends, and associates of Mr. Goines and the Goines family. Investigative research of the author's life was also used but was hindered in many cases because of the destruction of state and federal records, along with delays in compliance with requests for public information. In various places, dialogue is re-created based on recollections given during interviews.

I pray that this work accurately reflects the people, places, events, and accomplishments that characterized Mr. Goines's life. May it resonate in the hearts of his readers and admirers as confirmation of his intelligence and creative brilliance, in spite of his conspicuous flaws. May it be added unto the truth of his significance as one of the most important contributors to urban contemporary literature and popular culture.

Prelude: Death in Retrospect

The biggest, baddest, motherfuckin' gangster in history. That's who he'd wanted to be. Young men in his day dreamed of playing in the National Football League. Dreamed of signing a contract with Motown. Even dreamed of leading their people to freedom. He dreamed of being lawless and untouchable.

Eventually, he became the Godfather of display racks, bookshelves, and flashlights under children's bed covers. Now Donnie lay on his back, eyes closed, in a decorated casket, paperback novels tucked beneath his arms. The cause of death was a shotgun wound to the skull, an autopsy report stated. The back of Donnie's head had to be reshaped by morticians so his corpse looked more presentable.

It had been a very long thirty-seven years. Now, he would rest.

Sobs and organ music created eerie sounds around him. Several women buried their heads in the chests and shoulders of their husbands as they filed into the church, down the aisles, and to the place where his body rested. Donnie had touched some of them more deeply than their men previously knew. But absent from the services was Mary, the only woman who'd ever caused him to show himself emotionally vulnerable. A young prostitute, she'd become pregnant and pleaded with Donnie to let her give birth to the child, which she was confident belonged to him. Infuriated by the sentimentalism, he forced her to have an abortion. He believed in putting his bitches to work, and there was no such thing as maternity leave on Woodward Avenue.

She never survived the procedure. Never even left the clinic.

Two lives were cancelled, instead of one. Donnie agonized over his guilt. He hurt inside.

It was not long, though, before he was back on the streets with a vengeance. He went underground, where grief and sensitivity were weaknesses and ruthlessness was tantamount to survival. Raising hell became an art form when anyone crossed him. It was the only way to show nonbelievers who the fuck they were dealing with. It was the streets, ironically, that helped stage Donnie's brief but memorable literary career. It was the streets, ironically, that gave him the only legitimacy he ever enjoyed during his adult life.

In the end, however, as his mother, sisters, and a sanctuary filled with other friends, relatives, and admirers of his writing gathered in the east-side building to say good-bye, it was painfully obvious that the setting in his arena of experiences had changed. His corpse had been moved from a crime scene to a county medical examiner's office. From the church, it would be taken for burial at a sprawling cemetery in Warren, Michigan. With no headstone to identify it, even his place in the earth would become an obscurity. Weeds and untended growth would reach up to smother the tiny, concrete grave marker, just as demonlike distractions, temptations, and vices reached up from hellish places to smother his brilliance and potential.

Maturing

I remember that I was much too young when I first started reading his books, probably in the second or third grade. I recognized people in my neighborhood who were like the characters in his books.
—Robyn Ussery, enthusiast

Wham!

The shocked woman was stung from a blow to her face. A pretty, brown baby lay blanketed safely nearby in the snow, completely oblivious to the rage her mother directed at an unfortunate passerby who had stopped to admire the infant.

Wham!

Myrtle struck the bewildered woman again. It surely was not a scene one would have expected to witness in Evanston, Illinois, during the winter of 1934. Two white women fighting on a public street over a Negro baby? Actually, only Myrtle was fighting. The stranger was being thrashed. And actually, contrary to appearances, there was only one white woman. Blonde-haired, blue-eyed Myrtle was, perhaps, even more European in appearance than Claudette Colbert, the Paris-born movie star whose *Imitation of Life* was in theaters that year. It was entirely understandable, then, that the passerby made the mistake of commenting about Myrtle's firstborn in such an unflattering way. As Myrtle carried the baby wrapped tightly in a blanket to protect her from the extra chill blowing off of

Lake Michigan, the woman approached her, thinking that the three of them shared a common racial heritage. When she asked Myrtle to see the infant, Myrtle proudly parted the blanket to reveal her daughter Ceolia's bronze face.

For a second, the woman was taken aback.

"Oh," she said. "I've always wanted one for a pet."

After she'd gently placed the baby to the side, Myrtle commenced beating the hell out of the stranger. Under different circumstances, mother and daughter might have found their safety further jeopardized had anyone seen or gotten word of a nigger woman attacking a member of Evanston's more socially privileged class. As things resulted, though, the stranger was left simply stunned and in pain. Myrtle lifted her daughter off of the soft, white ground, brushed flakes from the blanket and continued on her way.

The son of a farmer, George Baugh married Clairette Ford in Little Rock, Arkansas, in 1899. They were both twenty-two years old. Born in 1909, Myrtle Baugh was the youngest of the couple's seven children. Another daughter, Arelia, died of a snake bite. The Baughs' combination of European, Native American, and African ancestry gave Myrtle and her siblings their fair, often misleading complexions. Across the state line east of Arkansas, Mississippi held a connection for the Baughs, whether real or imagined. Approximately 400 miles from Little Rock was the city of Biloxi. It was there, ten years before her birth, that a venerated and reviled figure—who would later be identified to Myrtle as an ancestor—died on the Beauvoir plantation. One of the key figures in the Civil War, Jefferson Davis had returned to Mississippi, following two years of imprisonment at Fort Monroe, Virginia, after his 1865 capture by Union Army troops. The surrender of Davis's best general, Robert E. Lee, a month earlier in Virginia had effectively ended the struggle between North and South. Davis, a former Mississippi senator who was elected president of the Confederate States of America in 1861, continued to advocate the right of eleven territories to secede from the Union until his death in 1889. Another right he advocated, like countless numbers of other southerners, was that of white land-owners to maintain slaves as property. Davis continued believing in Caucasian racial superiority long after his northern nemesis, Abraham Lincoln, issued the Emancipation Proclamation.

Myrtle and her siblings were told, however, that an enslaved woman called Fannie had been taken by the twice-married Davis as a concubine. They learned few details of any sort, whether Fannie had been taken by force or willingly, but were informed as fact that she bore a son and a daughter by the statesman. They were told the daughter, also named Fannie, was Clairette's mother. It was a curious thing to believe since no record of the servant Fannie appeared to exist in any of the Davis estate documents or in the will he left behind. Nonetheless, it would not have been the first time in the history of American chattel slavery that a plantation owner conceived with one of his servants. The absence of Fannie's name in Warren County, Mississippi, slave schedules or other property lists did not necessarily rule out her existence at the Davis estate, particularly since servants often were only identified by their numeric presence at the slave owner's residence. Neither proud, nor ashamed of their purported relation to one of the most infamous racists in history, the Baughs simply accepted his ancestry as a part of who they were. Myrtle would later tell her children about "old Jeff Davis" when discussing their lineage.

During Myrtle's childhood, Little Rock was not unlike many other southern cities. Segregation was the law of society. Arkansas Baptist College was the choice for advancement in higher education among the "colored" students of the city, while whites had various options. Agriculture was largely a way of life. Sharecropping was common in the black community. Often, farmers in the region tended what were called "truck patches," crop gardens designed not for distribution and profit but for the sustenance of individual families and households, which frequently contained hungry children. It wasn't uncommon for boys to be pulled out of school in the early grades, like third or fourth, in order to help work the soil at home. Girls generally attended classes a bit longer but were also required to assist with the crop gathering. Cotton was a primary source of the economy of the land. It had to be picked and chopped.

Life was a little different, however, for Myrtle and her siblings living in the Big Rock Township section of the city. George worked as a boilermaker and a porter, and Clairette, as a cook at a Little Rock Catholic school, then later a maid. Catholicism became a significant force in the lives and education of their children as well. Sadie, whom the family called Regina, Myrtle's oldest sister, found her way to Baltimore when she was about sixteen or seventeen years old. There, she joined a convent and eventually became a boarding-school teacher. George and Clairette put aside money to send Myrtle to attend classes there. It was a relatively stable existence the Baughs had managed to create for themselves and their offspring, considering that the parents were just one generation removed from slavery. Living in a former Confederate state that held folks like old Jeff Davis in great esteem made their modest achievements all the more remarkable. Like much of the region, Arkansas would demonstrate plenty of unbridled racism, some deadly, for years to come. Segregated streetcars and poll taxes designed to hinder the ability of blacks to vote were a part of the state's social legacy.

Many so-called colored folks might have viewed the Baugh family's mixed ancestry as a blessing in the clan's relative prosperity. Deceptively light-skinned and silky-haired, they could have easily opted to join that cadre of the black race that elected to pass. In fact, George's nephew Ford would become a police officer in Little Rock during the civil rights movement at a time when it violated segregation ordinances for him to be a member of the force. Probably more common than was ever discovered, passing was a method of virtual disappearance from the oppressed class achieved by those whose European physical appearance enabled them to join white citizens in their homes, churches, and places of work. Particularly during slavery and in the immediate postslavery era, terms like *mulatto, quadroon,* and *octoroon*—all designed as indicators of the amount of black blood in their overall genetic makeup— were used to describe people of mixed descent. Each member of the Baugh household, including George's mother, Sabre, had been identified as mulatto in the 1910 census, and Myrtle would come to accept the term in describing her family. How ridiculous, then, it would have seemed for a woman who fulfilled the necessary aesthetic criteria for passing to make rage on an unsuspecting stranger who'd unwittingly insulted her baby daughter. If there was any proclivity toward passing in the Baughs, however, it didn't seem to show itself. Their neighbors in Big Rock Township were black or of similarly mixed descent. They worked, worshipped, and socialized in the areas of Little Rock that found black presence acceptable. And perhaps it was for the best.

During the last six months of 1919, after the end of World War I, twenty-five race riots erupted in cities, both northern and southern, including tiny Elaine, Arkansas, not quite 100 miles outside Little Rock. That same year, nearly 100 people of color were lynched, commonly by hanging, a number of them veterans still in their uniforms. More than 360,000 black men had entered the military, many of those serving overseas in defense of a perceived American democracy. But, as with previous wars, upon their return and completion of duty, they held onto expectations of increased opportunities for themselves and their families. Instead what increased was the resentment of Caucasian citizens who no more intended to share their rights with niggers than they intended to share their wives. Mobs controlled cities for days, burning, flogging, shooting, and torturing their victims. Black men and women who showed any new inclination to retaliate or defend themselves were only met with an intensification of the white violence. Before the war, soldiers in Texas, located directly to the south of Arkansas, had caught plenty of hell. In 1906, after a group of ten to twenty unidentified men had fired their rifles into buildings near Fort Brown, an army base close to Brownsville, a police officer was wounded and a white bartender was killed. Without a hearing or anything that could be regarded as solid evidence, President Theodore Roosevelt dismissed 167 colored soldiers by means of dishonorable discharge. It would be sixty-six years later when a black congressman spurred a review of the case that resulted in honorable discharges for all of the men. Yet, by then, only one remained alive: an eighty-six-year-old named Dorsie Willis. He had spent the remainder of his life sweeping floors and giving shoe shines.

Living for the Baughs was, by comparison, uneventful, and they likely considered it a blessing. Myrtle enjoyed a relatively stable upbringing, in spite of the perils and hindrances of residing south of the Mason-Dixon. Few would have wondered what a railroad worker named Joseph Leonard Goines found appealing about Myrtle after she had matured into womanhood. Like the Baughs, Joe's family experienced marginalization in a white-dominated society. Their small hometown of Jellico in Tennessee, Arkansas's eastern neighbor state, bore no true resemblance to Little Rock's southern municipalism. Situated not far beneath the Kentucky border to its north and 66 miles outside of Knoxville, Jellico's population in 1900 was 1,283. It served as Campbell County's banking-post town. Joe, like Myrtle, was of mixed lineage, with ancestors who were African and Native American. But his rearing was not as comfortable as Myrtle's had been. Born in 1886, Joe lost his father Dudley in a coal-mining accident when he was still a boy. His mother, Julia, primarily raised him and his three brothers.

Joe matured and became rather industrious. With his red-brown skin and oily black hair, he determined that he would claim Spanish ancestry rather than endure the treatment blacks received at a time not long past the strained final years of Reconstruction. The federal government had attempted to help the nation recover from the Civil War, in the process providing new opportunities for the formerly enslaved population, often to the continued resistance of white southerners. At least seventy-four black lynchings, which commonly consisted of shooting, hanging, and burning victims, were recorded in the South the year of Joseph's birth. The Ku Klux Klan had been formed in Tennessee two decades earlier and made its terroristic presence felt there. But by 1892 when Joe turned six, black citizens of the state were responding to racial terror in more ways than one.

On March 9, 1892, three prominent businessmen were lynched in Memphis, far southwest of Jellico, after defending their store with guns when authorities colluded with a white competitor to close down the black-run establishment by force. "Tell my people to turn their faces West, for there is no justice for them here," were the last recorded words of Tom Moss, one of the lynching victims. A mass exodus of an estimated 6,000 Memphis residents to Oklahoma, which was among the newly opened Native American territories, followed the incident. Supported by the fiery journalist Ida B. Wells, who had been a friend to Moss, the departure was a major blow to the Memphis economy. But north of Jellico, several weeks before the Memphis residents began walking and traveling the 400-mile distance toward the former Cheyenne and Arapahoe reservations by whatever means available to them, black folks in Kentucky had also started to flee. Similar white terrorism had propelled their emigration, along with the western emigration of scores in Mississippi, Arkansas, and Georgia.

Joe would later decide as an adult that he wanted no part of this sort of reactionary survival. He legally changed the spelling of his surname, Goins, adding the letter *e* to give the impression that he was of Spanish rather than African descent. There was a chance, he figured, that it would be read and pronounced as "Goy-nez." If he were to catch hell as an English-speaking Spaniard, it would be a chance he was willing to take. Joe and his brothers left Tennessee when they reached their twenties, but they weren't headed farther south like many of the sojourners who evacuated the region in the years before them. Joe and Thomas traveled to Michigan, while their eldest siblings made it all the way to New York before settling. Joe had begun supporting himself by working as a Pullman porter. Now people of color were moving in droves for a different reason. Partly fueled by the start of World War I, industries in the North were experiencing a tremendous economic boost. Wages in the South at that time ranged from fifty cents to two dollars a day, while the northern states offered wages between two and five dollars daily. During the span of 1915–1920, between 500,000 and 1 million black men, women, and children made the trek to this Promised Land that stretched toward Canada.

By the time Joe met Myrtle in 1929, he had already married

once. A son, Ralph Goines, was the product of his first union. Myrtle had not long rejoined her family after leaving school in Baltimore when she found herself in the same city with the man who would become her husband. Her father had added his southern clan to the hundreds of thousands who participated in the Great Migration—the Baughs were now residents of Detroit. Myrtle had fallen in love with a soldier, but somehow their engagement was dissolved. When the goal-oriented Joe, who was twenty-three years her senior, took notice of the debutante, she was still relatively new to courting and relationships. No doubt, he regarded her blonde tresses and beige complexion as physical attributes. She would make a good companion for him. By midyear, George's youngest daughter had become Myrtle Goines. Joe and Myrtle found a home in a north Detroit neighborhood near the suburb of Hamtramck.

With Detroit's burgeoning reputation as the automobile capital of the world, factories created a demand for labor. Henry Ford had begun offering a five-dollar-a-day work shift to all employees, regardless of their color. The career opportunity, particularly as an alternative to sharecropping or domestic service, was appealing to many who remained in the southern states: The city's black community expanded from 5,000 residents in 1910 to 120,000 by 1930. But it wasn't all prosperous for the industrial workers as the years of the Great Depression collided with the Great Migration era. In fact, while Detroit was in the early stages of developing a black middle class, others who'd left their farms behind to seek urban stability could secure only low-wage jobs that limited their living options to crowded, low-rent districts that became ghettos. The October 1929 stock market crash devastated the national economy. In 1932, roughly half of the black laborers in Detroit, Chicago, New York, and Philadelphia found themselves out of work, with one of every three families receiving public assistance.

Despite the state of the national economy, an enterprising local group of Jewish young men were literally making a way for themselves. Detroit's near northwest side was known as Purple Gang territory. The fifty or so thugs who composed this mob earned their keep through contract murders, kidnappings, bootlegging, and selling their protection to businesses that looked to secure commercial assets. During the '20s and early '30s, Purples became notoriously familiar throughout the country as the goons who preyed upon the gangsters. When broadcaster Jerry Buckley had nerve enough to start naming members on the radio he got popped at the LaSalle Hotel. Chicago cops suspected Purples had served as the hit squad that whacked seven members of Bugs Moran's cartel in the blood-drenched St. Valentine's Day Massacre of 1929 as a professional service to Alphonse "Scarface" Capone. But the charge was unproven. Still, few would have disassociated the gang from the dozens of bodies that kept turning up in the Detroit River. That same year, federal agents reported that 85 percent of all illegal alcohol had entered the country along the same water route. Joe, who'd been making plans to go into more legitimate business for himself, determined that he and Myrtle would relocate to Evanston. The city's proximity to Chicago would likely reflect an urban environment well suited to his plans for building a customer base in dry cleaning. There, Joe and Myrtle began their family. On July 20, 1934, at 2:00 A.M. their first child Ceolia Marie Goines was born. She was named after an aunt on the Baugh side of her lineage. It had not been an easy birth for Myrtle. Clairette, who had joined her for the presentation of her granddaughter, complained to the hospital staff that they left Myrtle in labor for too long. But finally, Marie, as she would be called, was delivered following a cesarean procedure, as would be all of Myrtle's babies. Marie was a blessing to her mother, and Joe even treasured the little brown-skinned addition to their household, despite the fact that her appearance more closely resembled his than Myrtle's.

Within a year or so, the family moved again, this time to Chicago proper as Joe and Myrtle continued working to become successful in dry cleaning. Occasionally, Clairette would take the train from Detroit and fetch her grandbaby for visits while Joe and Myrtle operated the store, which was located in Chicago's South Side section. In 1936, Myrtle became pregnant again. This time, however, Clairette wasn't taking any chances with the hospitals or doctors who hadn't seemed to know what they were doing in Cook County. She apparently convinced her daughter to return to Detroit before having her second child. There, Clairette and George could see after her and help care for the newest Goines. That year, at 1:49 P.M. on December 15, Donald Joseph was born. Myrtle was twenty-seven. Joseph was fifty. Myrtle was thrilled to have a son. On the other hand, while he was much more fair in complexion than Marie, a middle name would prove to be nearly all he held in common with his father.

The Goines children would enjoy the same relative privilege that Myrtle and her siblings experienced in Little Rock. Marie was glad to have the company of a baby brother. The boy, who was given the nickname Donnie, would refer to her as "Wee Wee" when he was old enough to speak. In the earliest stages of their relationship Marie eased into her new big-sister role. One particular day, she was outside the house pushing Donnie in his carriage. In the span of a moment without supervision, her attention was distracted and the baby went rolling toward the street as a Chicago fire engine roared ahead. She never knew why, but though Marie was herself just a toddler, she suddenly had the presence of mind to turn around and quickly retrieve her brother. She gradually became a tiny yet reliable helper for Myrtle whenever Donnie needed watching. Meanwhile, the Goines family wasn't the only one expanding. Myrtle's sister Elsie D and brother George began bringing their children to Chicago from Detroit for regular visits with their cousins. Doris and Catherine were among the younger relatives who kept Marie company, though Doris thought Marie to be a "selfish little bitch" where their conflicting play habits were concerned.

While her socialization continued at home, eventually it was time for Marie to enter kindergarten. One incident in school gave the child what was perhaps her first lesson about race and the strange dynamics of color within her family. After all, she had a father who tried to avoid being identified with black folks—who thanked God every day for Marie's thin lips and small nose—and a mother who was willing to throttle white folks who might perceive Myrtle as being like them. How, then, was she to associate herself? The answer became either stunningly clear or all the more confusing the day Myrtle showed up to retrieve her from class. Finding herself at a loss to locate Mrs. Goines's daughter, the teacher informed Myrtle of her quandary. Only then did the mother realize the teacher had gone looking for a little white child before finally releasing Marie to her custody. Marie would never forget the day she and her doting mother were treated as complete strangers to one another.

Just two years behind her, Donnie appeared to be growing into a rather typical boy. It was only fitting that he would lop off his sister's long, beautiful braids one day when they were outside "playing Indians." It was also only fitting that Joe and Myrtle would go out and raise a hearty fuss about it. They preferred that the children recognize their Native American ancestry in other ways. About 1940, wanderlust kicked in once more. Joe and Myrtle shut down the cleaning store, packed up the children, and returned to Detroit, this time to stay. They briefly lived with George and Clairette before settling into a house at 13953 St. Aubin on the city's northeast side. There, they were surrounded by relatives from both Joe's and Myrtle's families. Joe set up shop nearby on Victor Street. He called the new business Northside Cleaners. Meanwhile, Thomas Goines had also ventured into dry cleaning with his own establishment in the area of historic Fort Wayne. But he just barely got out alive when the boiler in his building exploded. Tom lost fingers and his ears burned off, leaving him permanently deformed after a stay in the hospital.

Various primarily European ethnic groups had inhabited the city since Frenchman Antoine de la Mothe Cadillac founded Detroit nearly 250 years before the Goines clan decided to backtrack. German immigrants established the Sacred Heart Catholic School sometime after Sacred Heart parish opened in 1875. Located at 970 Eliot, the school was for students in kindergarten through eighth grade. In 1938 Edward Mooney, who was an archbishop at the time, designated Sacred Heart the facility where black parishioners could send their sons and daughters to be educated. The Catholic Church didn't formally support racial segregation, yet students were expected to attend classes at their assigned locations, which would not have qualified as ethnically diverse. In 1939 Holy Ghost was constructed from the ground as a second school to which the archbishop assigned students of color.

Donnie was admitted to Sacred Heart kindergarten on September 2, 1941. His birthday still months away, he was a four-year-old student among his school peers. He started in Room 101 and remained there until the end of first grade. By then World War II had begun, ushering in a renewal of the mass migration to Detroit as the city became known as the "Arsenal of Democracy." Production of war supplies led to $14 billion in contracts—approximately 10 percent of the nation's battle spending—which resulted in an increase of available factory positions. The region's population increased by about 300,000 within only four years. As the constituency of southeastern Michigan's broader territory grew, within a decade Detroit's black population had doubled to 200,000 by 1943. Caucasian resentment about the location of a city housing project in a white neighborhood, expressed in cross burning and other hateful acts, provided a disturbing resemblance to the South for many transplanted opportunity-seekers who thought they'd left behind the days of being unable to live comfortably in their God-given skin. In an act of defiance toward whites and as a statement of retaliation against unfair conditions, some initiated a "bumping campaign," through which they would deliberately walk into white folks on the street, knocking them off sidewalks or nudging them in elevators. Nationally distributed *Life* magazine likened the situation in Detroit to dynamite. Shortly thereafter, the city exploded in a way that proved the accuracy of *Life*'s reporting.

Tension related to the increased competition for jobs, housing, and educational opportunities was probably a primary factor. Those who were irritated by the influx of newcomers and the hustle for advancement took to referring to their city as "the arsehole of democracy." Then there was the 200-person battle royal on Belle Isle Park that followed an incident involving two black men who'd shown up behaving rather aggressively toward white visitors in response to their ejection from Eastwood Park five days earlier. And there was false information: incendiary lies about attacks on innocent citizens that never took place. The combination of dangerous elements developed into thirty-six hours of race rioting, shooting, and marauding like Detroit had never seen. Policemen were shot, stores were looted, blacks were attacked as they descended from streetcars, and an Italian doctor, Joseph De Horatiis, was killed after he disregarded police warnings and responded to a house call in a black neighborhood. Ultimately, federal troops were called in, and armored cars and Jeeps carrying automatic rifles rolled down Woodward, Detroit's main drag in and out of town. In addition to the dozens killed, more than 1,800 people were arrested.

"They have treated the Negroes terribly," William Guther told the media, referencing the police department's lily-white force of 3,400 officers. "They have gone altogether too far."

Guther's reaction to the bigoted rage and hostility was all the more significant, considering that he was an army brigadier general who had been charged with supervising the troops dispatched to Detroit to help quell the uprising. Close to 300 similar racial disturbances took place that same summer in forty-seven other cities, including Mobile, Alabama, and Harlem. The tone for five more decades of continued social fear, ignorance, and ethnic intolerance throughout America had, in effect, been set. The Goines home prospered while the nation went about the business of war and its communities stood nakedly vulnerable to spontaneous combustion. They were the first in the neighborhood to purchase a car and the first to bring a television into their living room. Between long hours of work, Joe and Myrtle partied hard with their in-laws and siblings. Myrtle enjoyed sipping Canadian whiskey; Joe liked the sport of betting. On Sundays he and Tom would regularly take the children to a bar on Dequindre, which was owned by a woman. The brothers kept cash. They even wore their money belts as they played games like five-card stud and tonk. With hundred-dollar bills stacked like Monopoly money, they encouraged the children to gamble. Marie would usually sit on Tom's lap, while Donnie stayed near his father. Oftentimes, after they'd played their hands, the men let Donnie and Marie keep their winnings and gave them fare for a matinee movie.

Goineses—or Goinses—and Baughs occupied four houses in a row on St. Aubin. When Regina came home from the convent she stayed with Joe and Myrtle in an upstairs room. Holidays for the family resembled country-style feasts and celebrations that might have made the former Baugh neighbors in Little Rock envious. Joe and Tom found hogs to slaughter and have the women prepare. The ladies made sausage from the fresh meat. Joe and Myrtle would drink spirits together until they were pleasantly intoxicated, as they occasionally did after slipping away into the dry cleaners after business hours. In the warmer months, they would take the children horseback riding in nearby Canada. Theirs was a kind of life experience that had always seemed reserved for others of a caste that was self-selected for favor and advantage. It appeared to be a great beginning for a little boy who enjoyed lemon meringue pie to grow into a happy, successful young man.

Third times proved not to be the charm for Donnie early on, as he was held back to repeat grade three at Sacred Heart. Just weeks after the New Year on January 28, 1946, he began attending classes in the Detroit Public Schools system, leaving behind the nuns who'd served as his instructors. Inside the walls of Davison Elementary he would continue his education, but like a few of his cousins Donnie was assigned to the "open-air" section because of a spot on his lungs. By now the family had moved to Dequindre Road near Davison Avenue on a tract of land where both the house and their new cleaning facility were located.

Many of the public schools in the area were enrolled with a sizable population of immigrant students, some of whom had not yet adjusted to American culture. Administrative records indicated each child's birth country as well as the birthplace of his or her parents and the language spoken at home. About 300,000 of the city's nearly 2 million people were foreign born. In adjacent Highland Park there were a good number of Irish, and neighboring

Hamtramck was mainly Polish. Canadians, Italians, Germans, and others new to the country had also settled in the area in their search for security during the evolving auto age.

Donnie more or less struggled in the classroom all the way through his years at Cleveland, the junior high school where he enrolled in 1949. Whether he had particular learning problems or simply failed to apply himself, he apparently earned only two As during all three of his years at Cleveland, both in the seventh grade for a class called Household Mechanics. In English he earned mostly Cs and Ds; social science, Ds; math, more Ds; and general science and first aid he ultimately failed, due to lack of hours. Donnie also took elective-type courses like art, swimming, and drafting but evidently had little interest. Where he did find stimulation was on the baseball field. He preferred the use of Cleveland's diamond to its classrooms. Donnie developed into a talented athlete, a left-handed pitcher who dreamed of playing in the majors. The Detroit Tigers had recently played their first night game before 54,480 spectators at Briggs Stadium, and Jackie Robinson's 1947 integration of the league as a Brooklyn Dodgers outfielder generated excitement in black communities nationally.

Oddly, Joe Goines had taken to keeping company with another prominent black sports hero. Joe Louis retired after seventeen years as the world's heavyweight boxing champion the same year that Donnie first walked through the doors of Cleveland. Louis, who had become a legitimate American hero after defeating the Adolf Hitler–endorsed Max Schmeling in a rematch bout, was, like Joe, a transplanted southerner who had moved to Detroit during the Great Migration. However the two Joes got to know one another, clearly the drycleaner put aside his disassociation from Negroes long enough to develop their friendship. Louis was among the most recognizable black men anywhere in the world and took pride in his race. Conscious of stereotypes, the boxer refused to be photographed while eating watermelon, an image that he knew could be misinterpreted as primitive or undignified. After meeting John Roxborough, a street-wise numbers runner and businessman, along with Roxborough's partner, Julian Black, he had managers who'd advised him about his public conduct. The Brown Bomber avoided drinking, smoking, and being spotted with white women. Though Louis's nightlife was active—including courtships with ladies, both black and white—his gentlemanly and humble ways gained him popularity, even among white southerners who condescendingly viewed the champ as nonthreatening. Donnie and Marie enjoyed visiting Louis's land in the outlying areas of the city. In such company, there was little reason to wonder why they were seen as the "rich kids" among their peers in the extended family. Joe would often take Myrtle and the children to visit there. They had drinks under a veranda, rode horses, and enjoyed fine company.

But life wasn't all recreation for the Goines kids. Donnie and Marie were responsible for helping at the cleaners on weekends and on weekday evenings after school. The newest store also had an on-site plant, which enabled Joe to treat his customers' laundry without leaving the premises. Delivery and retrieval service was the only thing where work was concerned that truly made it necessary for Joe and his assistants to stray from home at all. Joe drove a route out into the rural areas of southeast Michigan, removing clothes for return and loading others onto a pickup truck. Further out, he had mostly white customers, who seemed all too pleased to give him their business, while his black clientele was in the city. When Marie became old enough, he taught her to drive, and she would help him make the rounds. Eventually, Joe shut down the Victor Street location as the Dequindre store became the lifeblood of the Goines's sustenance.

It was not long, however, before Donnie's disinterest in supporting the family business began to surface. As his parents worked and played hard, he became disturbed when they didn't attend school functions or baseball games in which he took part. Perhaps it didn't seem to Donnie that his father was enthused about him. Far from an affectionate sort of dad, Joe preferred to let his actions as a provider speak for themselves. On the other hand, he was partial to his daughter and made it quite obvious. His oldest girl was his joy; though he didn't express it with hugs and kisses, some of his broadest smiles were reserved for Marie. Now Myrtle was a different story. She surely loved her daughter, but Donnie would always be her boy. If her husband wouldn't show it, she could be proud for both of them. Donnie's perceptions, nonetheless, were forming in ways that would be difficult to reverse. Before he turned sixteen, in what would seem like the span of only a few moments, Myrtle's boy would make a decision to alter the course of his entire life.

War

With a vigorous shove, Jessie started me towards the door. I ran out of the shop into the street I loved so well. There was not much difference between the daylight business and the night business on Hastings. The street was full of slow-moving cars, the drivers being more interested in the colored prostitutes in the doorways than on the traffic moving in front of them.

—*Whoreson,* Donald Goines

Hudson's department store was a symbol of Detroit prosperity as the 1950s began. The towering structure employed hundreds of workers and drew multitudes of shoppers. Store executives reported million-dollar sales days on at least two occasions. Hudson's five restaurants served something in the neighborhood of 14,000 meals on a daily basis. Negroes were limited to work as kitchen help; women, generally fair-complexioned, were paid as elevator operators. The store became the center of a bustling downtown. The city's most prominent black neighborhood had been thriving as well. East of downtown was the self-contained Black Bottom community. Coincidentally named for the dark texture of its soil during the nineteenth century, Black Bottom was a virtual network for entrepreneurs of color. Though some of the residential sections resembled slums, with ragged houses and outdoor toilets, Black Bottom functioned as an empowerment zone without the benefit of federal dollars and designations. A city within a city, the neighborhood and its residents exuded a pride and devotion that belied any suggestion by white society that they were second-class citizens.

Black Bottom produced men and women of character and determination. Its businesses and institutions, which included a breadth of service provision, left little need for any form of reliance on sources outside the community. For food and necessities, there were grocery stores. For recreation, pool halls could be found with little effort. For information, newspapers were published and distributed. Accountants set up shop in the area. Even deaths and funerals could be handled by a number of Black Bottom's mortuaries. And there was also entertainment. That was one area where the neighborhood was without rival anywhere within the city limits or in most of the Midwest. Paradise Valley was just about the liveliest spot around. Hastings Street, lined with every imaginable establishment, was the main drag through the community. There were twenty-four-hour movie theaters that offered admission for a few dimes and restaurants where it was said that the cooking oil flavored all of the entrees. No matter what a patron ordered, the meal was often reported to have the savor of fish. One of the most popular places to eat was Perkins, while Brosche's was known for its tasty biscuits.

Jazz royalty like Dinah Washington, Ella Fitzgerald, and bluesy Billie Holiday took to the stages of nightclubs in the Paradise Valley district. The pains of poverty, abuse, and drug addiction could be heard in Holiday's high-pitched vocals. Bandleader Duke Ellington surely thrilled crowds when he and his orchestra took their "A Train" through the Valley, performing the signature Billy Strayhorn collaboration to the joy of audiences who loved the blaring horns and multi-instrumental sound. And who would have been fool enough to miss a Cab Calloway performance? In his signature white tux with flowing tails, Calloway was the personification of style. The self-fashioned vocalist and showman told Detroiters all about "Minnie the Moocher" in his animated and often humorous delivery.

> *She ran around with a cat named Smokey*
> *She loved him, though he was cokey*

Further elaborating on poor Minnie's misfortunes with her cocaine-addicted lover, Calloway sang to the crowd of how Smokey

Joe took her to Chinatown and "showed her how to kick the gong around"—a coded reference to smoking opium. The performer delighted, as always, in hearing the crowd join in with his call-and-response:

> *Hi de hi de hi de hi!*
> *["Hi de hi de hi de hi!"]*
>
> *Hey de hey de hey de hey!*
> *["Hey de hey de hey de hey!"]*

Along with appearances by such top-shelf national and local performers of the day, to accompany the Harlem-like nightlife of Paradise Valley, there were welcoming bars like the Flame Show and the 606 Horseshoe Lounge. Out-of-towners could even stretch out at hotels like the Dewey, the Biltmore, the Norwood, or Mark Twain. But by 1950 the look of the neighborhood had begun to change. Named for a member of the prestigious family that established the thriving automobile company, the Edsel Ford Freeway was constructed. The Ford was built through Black Bottom's boundaries, and more of the area was obliterated in 1953 when the John C. Lodge Freeway opened. About 17,000 residents were displaced. A few years later, city officials would choose to build Interstate 75 over Hastings Street. The sights and sounds of Paradise eventually gave way to the capitalism and convenience of white urban renewal.

Life was largely a hustle for more than a handful of black men and women in the larger cities of America. In fact, for those who saw too much distance between their education, talents, or training and the requirements of a prohibitive establishment, hustlin' became a career. And it seemed there was always a hustle to be found in the ghetto; in the lower echelon; in the shadow of space and time that left just enough room to walk the line between what was legal and what was necessary. Generally, what was legal wound up stepped on. Although Black Bottom was populated with legitimate, decent, working-class people, there were also the familiar characters who decorated the corner landscape of every other urban center. They might have discreetly held onto something for protection but were generally nonviolent and thought harmless to anyone not interested in what they had to offer. Hustlers like the pimp and the prostitute, the street peddler, the numbers runner. What Donnie lacked in study skills and book knowledge he recovered in less legitimate talents. He observed the various street hustles and developed a knack for card games and shooting craps. As a small-time gambler, he discovered a way to keep pocket money for himself, and it had nothing to do with cleaning other men's funky underwear. It was somewhere near the time he'd reached the eighth grade when he appeared to recognize this alternative lifestyle option. In spite of the Catholic school education, the respectable mother and father, and the stability that came with being the heir to a family business, Donnie had begun to feel the pull of the street. After all, the North End, where the Goines residence was located, wasn't too far from Black Bottom.

Donnie began trading his deficient self-esteem as initiation to the world. Never particularly vain, he had not thought of himself as being attractive or otherwise. In large part, through the bluntness of his peers, however, he had become acutely sensitive about his complexion. Unlike in the South, where its significance was emphasized through omnipresent signs, such as NO DOGS, NO COLOREDS, Detroit segregation was less declarative. Yet, despite the headlines and current events that reflected the discrimination surrounding him, Donnie developed his greatest sense of race and place among his own people. It might have seemed inevitable, considering Joe's idiosyncrasies and Myrtle's intriguing ethnic background, that Donnie agonized about his physical appearance, mainly the lightness of his skin. Marie would observe his pale hands as they worked side by side in the cleaning store. One of their duties was to handle men's pants, turning the pockets and cuffs inside out. *He looks just like Momma,* Marie would think to herself, comparing her milky caramel complexion to his. She never teased him about it, though. Never called her brother "high yellow," "red," or any of the abusive names she' heard the neighborhood' boys use to characterize his paleness or the rouge undertones that reflected his Native American heritage. A lot of Donnie's cohorts were likely jealous, having been programmed through television and billboard ads to believe that the closer you were to white, the prettier you were. Like Myrtle, whose broad nose was perhaps the only feature that distinguished her as a person of color, Donnie fit well with what often was regarded as the most enviable image of blackness. After all, fair-skinned, Brooklyn-born Lena Horne was among the few people of color to project an image of elegance and glamour in the mass media as she gave memorable performances on film screens; the similarly hued, slick-haired Calloway was cast in several parts that allowed him to show off his swingin' style in front of the camera. Yet, there were no movie contracts or cameras rolling for ordinary, twelve-year-old, high-yellow kids in Detroit. Not even the ones with Donnie's silklike "good" hair.

It was, at least partly then, due to the self-esteem issues associated with his complexion that Donnie began using delinquent behavior to assimilate. It was during the time when he was enrolled at Cleveland. Away from the stinging rulers of the nuns who enforced zero-tolerance discipline in the classroom. Away from the closely monitored hallways and catechism principles. Where Donnie had found the nerve was another question entirely. He only figured that his willingness to run with the crew would assure his acceptance. Nerve would be the attribute that diverted the attention often focused on his sallow countenance. He would be relieved of merciless taunting. As much as those words hurt, Donnie might have chosen to suffer a physical beating instead.

Even as Donnie began to succumb to peer pressures, he remained fairly stable in his development as a young man, at least to the casual observer. He liked to shoot his mock rifle and pass time with his cousins. Along with Myrtle and Marie, he continued attending Mass and taking Sunday communion. Though Joseph wasn't much of a churchgoer, he volunteered every summer to drive the Sacred Heart parish sisters out to the country where they had their retreats. In March 1949 Donnie entered a speech class at Cleveland, and he dropped his shop course in order to work more at the cleaners. If Joe and Myrtle suspected their only son was slipping from them, they never showed it. The thought never entered their minds that within the next two years he would be living as a full-grown man thousands of miles away.

Donnie's shy but charming smile was surely an attraction to the female students at Pershing High School, where he was admitted in 1951. In his few years as a student at Cleveland, he missed nearly seventy days of class. At Pershing, another public school located on the east side, he continued to go through the motions. It was around this time that Marie began to take an interest in the study of dance. Freshman class member Donnie, on the other hand, found nothing Pershing offered to be of any particular interest. His bonds with the friendly, young, neighborhood criminals, meanwhile, appeared to grow stronger. Riff raff was their specialty, and Donnie played a part in creating it. The words that had previously crushed him, driven him into an ever-present state of self-consciousness, seemed to matter little now. Hell, they were all just little niggers anyway. At least as far as the white folks and the strangers were concerned. So what difference did their shades make, really? Sensing that Donnie needed some sort of private space as he matured into adulthood, Joe made an uncharacteristically thoughtful gesture on the teenager's behalf. He constructed a recreation room above the cleaning plant. He bought a billiards table and opened the space for Donnie to entertain. He and Marie would frequently welcome their nearby cousins and friends from the block up to their little quarters. But Donnie soon developed other ideas about how Joe's rare gift could be used.

Marie watched the scene in amazement. If she had ever doubted that her little brother knew how to find ways to create trouble for himself, well, now she was a believer. She had no idea where it came from. No idea how they'd gotten hold of it. No ideas about anything except the fact that she was actually seeing it, right there in the rec room: Donnie and the gang had actually stolen a safe. These teenagers were in possession of a storage vessel for valuable, possibly even priceless, items. How they'd actually gotten it down the street and through the door would have been too much to ponder.

Would they be arrested? Would someone try to kill her brother? Had it been stolen from the home of an elderly person who wouldn't know how to survive without its contents? Marie wondered to herself but never quite found the courage to ask. She wasn't even sure she wanted to know. Donnie was becoming bolder and bolder in his lawlessness. To be certain, it could no longer be considered simply mischievous or playful. He and the gang handed Marie a twenty-dollar bill from the safe box. Whether it was to celebrate their crime, to ensure her silence, or simply to calm her obviously frazzled young nerves, she was uncertain. As she watched the band of thieves peering and reaching into the open metal door, she thought only of the solemn truth that things would probably not get better where her brother's descent into juvenile delinquency was concerned. If he would participate in a heist like this, what wouldn't he do? Since they were babies, separated by an insignificant number of years, they had been each other's first real friends. But Donnie was far from an infant. In fact, he was charging recklessly toward the dangerous consequences that came along with being a certain kind of man. If Myrtle ever found out what he was doing, it would only break her heart, Marie knew. She was frightened, but nothing seemed like the right thing to do. It may well have been that nothing was.

Grade nine at Pershing would be Donnie's last year of school. The world around him was preparing for a change, and he would soon find himself in the midst of a personal transformation. As early as May 1950, President Harry S. Truman had received word that Negroes in the navy were "completely integrated with whites in basic training, technical schools, on the job, in messes and sleeping quarters, ashore and afloat." Three years earlier in July, Truman became responsible for the executive order that "there shall be equality of treatment and opportunity for all persons in the armed services without regard to race, color, religion or national origin." Top military brass feared public reaction and kept any report of the presidential mandate from the newspapers but accepted their instructions nevertheless. Members of Congress kept the code of silence. It would be well into the new decade before the effects of the policy became generally known. About three-fourths of the blacks in the U.S. Air Force had been integrated into 1,301 mixed Negro and white units, and all of its schools and jobs had been made accessible to all races. The army was slower in its progress than the other branches, however, until the summer of 1950, when a surplus of black troops in Korea was combined with a shortage of Caucasian soldiers. The black servicemen were called upon as the solution to a mounting problem of American casualties during the war crisis. A regimental commander felt compelled to integrate them with his depleted white platoons. The Negro squadrons shined. They fought even more effectively than they had previously.

Korea came under Japanese control in 1895 and was made part of the larger island territory in 1910. Allied forces defeated Japan during World War II, however, and U.S. and Soviet squads moved into Korea. The United Nations General Assembly had declared in 1947 that elections should be held throughout the nation so one government could be chosen, but the Soviets resisted and would not allow the elections to take place in the northern part of the country. It was the first instance in history in which a world organization would play a military role. The UN had been in existence for only five years.

The ensuing war was the first in which jet aircraft battles took place. Initially, Allied bombers and fighter planes supported the ground troops, killing enemy soldiers and damaging their bases. Then the Soviet Union began providing North Korea with planes and so-called "dogfights" became a part of the conflict. In the dogfights, which occurred above North Korea, close to 300,000 Communist troops were killed. Yet, with all the developments and dimensions of the war being waged overseas, back in the States, there was more of a metaphoric battle between communism and capitalism being waged. As the focus of antagonism between Russia and America shifted to other Asian territory, it became apparent that the two powers were facing off in an ideological struggle for world domination. Communists had used stories of color discrimination and social injustice to discredit Western capitalism and so-called democracy for some time. Against such a backdrop, the matter of racial segregation became international in its scope, as daily news in Tokyo, Saigon, Peiping, and Delhi was examined by the U.S. State Department for reactions to explosions of black and white violence in places like the Goines clan's home state or Florida.

One item that would not likely have been regarded newsworthy in the eastern press pertained to a brief filed at the U.S. Supreme Court in late 1952. The filing pertained to cases involving segregation in public schools and included a statement from the attorney general:

> It is in the context of the present world struggle between freedom and tyranny that the problem of racial discrimination must be viewed . . . Racial discrimination furnishes grist for the Communist propaganda mills, and it raises doubt even among friendly nations as to the intensity of our devotion to the democratic faith . . . The segregation of school children on a racial basis is one of the practices in the United States, which has been singled out for hostile foreign comment in the United Nations and elsewhere. Other peoples cannot understand how such a practice can exist in a country which professes to be a staunch supporter of freedom, justice and democracy.

While statements referencing the "struggle between freedom and tyranny" were surely confusing to black folks who couldn't tell the difference between Communist tyrants and so-called democratic ones—especially black folks who had the prior year's lynching fresh in memory—the government's paranoia was comforting. Along with helping to monitor world peace and military aggression, the new United Nations functioned as an open curtain to the stage of America's domestic policies and practices. Word of Jim Crow segregation laws came as a total shock to many of the delegates from foreign countries who came to the United States, where UN headquarters was established. Among delegates who had heard anything about the system before traveling to America, stories of race restriction and subjugation were often dismissed, but now they witnessed it in action on a daily basis. Still more significant were the UN committees of investigation and their published reports, along with debates that generated unflattering portraits of the moral code in the land of the free. This caused genuine embarrassment to the State Department, which attempted to recover by making high-profile appointments of Negroes to Foreign Service positions. But none of the tokenism and face-saving effort translated into any form of change in the lifestyles or setbacks of the masses in Detroit, Chicago, New York, St. Louis, Atlanta, Birmingham, Houston, and elsewhere.

Communism had begun to spread its intentions in the black community decades earlier. Officially founded in 1921, the Communist Party of the United States of America was formed out of several splinter groups that emerged from the left wing of the Socialist Party. The party's platform argued that "the interests of the Negro worker are identical with those of the white," insisting that the plight of the race was inseparable from the class struggle. Subscribers to communism created agitation for the government, which was particularly uneasy about the impact this ideology might have among black intellectuals and black labor leaders. Many early black Communist converts were former supporters of Marcus Garvey's Universal Negro Improvement Association or similar nationalist movements. Gradually, the philosophy also began to attract members of the arts and cultural community. Communist cultural critics collected black folks' music and began writing jazz reviews. And one especially high-profile court case involving American racism, which was litigated in various phases from 1931 to 1950, created a window of opportunity for the Communist Party to express its support for the black cause in concrete, ass-bearing, put-up-or-shut-up fashion. Nine black young men, ranging in age from thirteen to twenty, were arrested on a freight train after several young whites complained that they had been thrown off in

Paint Rock, Alabama. Also on the train were two Caucasian women, who were taken with the blacks to the town of Scottsboro. After first denying that any assault had taken place on the train, with pressure from a lynch mob, they agreed to say they had been raped, despite two doctors' exams that found no evidence. After poorly run trial proceedings, tainted in every phase by racism, the all-white, all-male jury returned a verdict, finding each of the nine defendants guilty and voting for a straight ticket of death sentences, with the exception of the youngest.

Before the trials concluded, a Communist-fronted legal organization called the International Labor Defense had sent a telegram to the judge demanding a change of venue; urged on by a town prosecutor, a lynch mob had spilled into the streets on the very first night the men spent in Scottsboro's jail. Following eyewitness observation of the trial by two members, one black, the Communist Party decided to take up the defense of the accused men. The organization's involvement ultimately transformed what would have been an ordinary matter of court-approved nigger-lynching into a case that drew national attention. Not only did they provide experienced lawyers during appeals of the verdicts, but they staged protests in many northern cities, and in conjunction with supporters in London, Moscow, and elsewhere, even coaxed one of the alleged victims into attending a rally after she recanted her previous testimony. Well-known Detroit Communist leader Carl Winter helped arrange for one of the accused men to take refuge on a tract of land in Michigan after he had escaped from the custody of a prison farm. As the years progressed, charges were dropped against the four youngest defendants, with the others receiving reduced sentences. By the time the last man received his freedom, they had spent a combined total of 100 years in the jails and penitentiaries of Alabama.

The nation's anxiety about communism was embodied in the creation of the House Committee on Un-American Activities, which announced that it would hold hearings to investigate the loyalty of its more suspect citizens. The committee made its presence felt in Detroit, though perhaps not with the results it sought.

On February 28, 1952, a thirty-four-year-old labor activist made a name for himself when members came to investigate local Communists. Coleman A. Young would later become the city's first black mayor, but now he would put on a show that the House Committee members would've preferred to forget. Communists had been highly visible in Detroit through the years, attracting 50,000 people downtown in one earlier protest against unemployment. As they did elsewhere, the faithful led efforts to eliminate Detroit segregation but also to end harassment in the workplace and reduce evictions. With the auto plants and the city's other industrial enterprises combined, there was a powerful job union. Party supporters sought a means by which they could penetrate it, suggesting that the principles of organizing in the workplace were compatible with Communist philosophy. Yet, like the federal officials, local authorities held little tolerance for such thought, which they regarded as left-wing bullshit. Police officers on horseback had responded to the downtown protest by busting heads, sending two dozen of the demonstrators to the hospital.

So it wouldn't have been advantageous to find oneself publicly regarded as a Communist and even less so if one were a Negro. Albert Cobo, who occupied the mayor's office for most of the '50s, and at the time when Detroit reached its peak population of 1.825 million, already had played on Caucasian fears about their restive black cohabitants. It was with certainty, then, that Young would be regarded an "uppity nigger" once his Un-American Activities hearing took place. Although the committee generally intimidated witnesses called to testify about their political bent, Young took control of his interview from the start. He tore into a House Committee lawyer for "slurring" the word *Negro* into the derogatory-sounding "nigra." Like the multitalented Communist Negro actor Paul Robeson, Young was defiant as a witness, and he chose to be a motherfucker about it. "You must have me mixed up with a stool pigeon," he told committee members who asked him for information about colleagues who belonged to the National Negro Labor Council, which he founded. A native of Tuscaloosa, Alabama, Young was uncontrollable, even going as far as lecturing the board's southern chairman about how his time would be better spent investigating the denial of voting and civil rights to blacks in other parts of the country. The confrontational hearing helped begin a contentious relationship of government investigation and surveillance of Young's life and political career that would last another forty years.

At 13224 Dequindre, war, communism, and politics were possibly the lowest items on one young man's list of personal concerns. Trouble stayed on Donnie's mind—specifically, making it. But as he grew older, his cravings for new experiences and adventures exceeded that which his peers in the gang could provide. On the safer side, Donnie was given an opportunity to play the role of elder sibling, as had Marie with him. Joe and Myrtle had begun raising their third and last child when Joan was born in 1948. With her mother not quite forty and her father a ripe sixty-two years of age, little Joanie could have benefited from Donnie's supplemental supervision and guidance during her early years. They bonded, indirectly, when Marie, who had prayed for a baby sister, occasionally pushed Joanie in her carriage to the diamond where they watched Donnie play baseball. Still, Donnie's affection for the new baby proved to be small comfort to him. Little "Poopty" would be just fine without him. Donnie pondered his options. Having no use for the curriculum at Pershing High or any additional needs that could be fulfilled by the crew from which he once sought acceptance, the notion struck him: There was a way that he could leave home, avoid having to hear any more of Joe's bullshit about working at Northside, and experience life, all at the same time. Donnie would join the military. But at just fifteen, his juvenile status would make that impossible. How could he do it? He pondered again. Running the streets had taught him at least one thing that school never did—the importance of improvising. If ever he had been caught laying game on a fool, it would have been his undoing. Clearly, any sensible plan always had to include a willingness to change plans if necessary. Thinking the plot through, however, Donnie decided that his initial preference could work after all. Without being detected, he managed to get his deceiving hands on Marie's birth certificate. His sister had already graduated and gone on traveling in her career as a stage dancer. He altered it convincingly. So much so that it now listed Donald Joseph Goines's year of birth as 1934.

Not long afterward, news came to the family that Donnie had enlisted with the U.S. Air Force. Joe certainly didn't fall to pieces. By contrast, Myrtle was heartbroken. What made him run away? Where would he be stationed? Would he be able to survive the Korean War? Questions lingered for weeks as acceptance sunk in that they might not see their only son again for years, if ever. As to Donnie's motive in making such a drastic choice, speculation was the only route that could be taken. Some in the family heard that Joe had been abusive toward him. Knocked Donnie around from time to time. Years later, Donnie would tell at least one friend he had been molested. But there was no children's agency to investigate such claims if there had been attempts to report them. Furthermore, it was tough to imagine Donnie being disciplined or handled inappropriately without his mother raising hell about it, if she knew. She was a dutiful and supportive wife, but—as the woman on that street in Evanston learned—she could be fierce in matters that involved her children. Let alone that Myrtle was no shrinking violet when it came to confrontations with her husband. Joe would flirt from time to time, and he found out how Myrtle felt about it on the occasion when she attacked him after finding Joe in a parked car with a white woman. Mama didn't take no mess, so why her boy left was a puzzler. Perhaps Donnie had heard news of MacArthur's flawed prediction that the war wouldn't last long and thought his enlistment was a safe decision. Perhaps the thought of dropping bombs or driving a tank overseas had thrilled him in that boyish, foolish way that made the bloody battle seem genuinely appealing. Whatever his perceptions, Donnie was clearly no longer the same kid who had expressed desires to become a professional ball player, throwing strikes over home plate as filled stadiums adored him. As easily as he could be fitted for a uniform, his field of dreams would become a field of battle.

If it had been his goal to get out of the neighborhood, he achieved it exceptionally. Donnie first found himself stationed in Japan as the war continued. If anyone suspected that he was only a school-aged child, they apparently never voiced it. Donnie assimilated to military discipline and culture well enough to avoid drawing much attention to himself early on. His adjustment was likely not much more of a stretch than his leap from privileged Catholic boy to wayward high school dropout had been, only in reverse. Here, he would have to prove he was a man. He would be responsible for directing the course of his life. Like others from throughout the country, Detroiters found themselves on the front lines of battle. Marine Robert Simanek, of suburban Farmington Hills, was given the Medal of Honor after his unit was ambushed in Korea during the summer of 1952. Having suffered heavy casualties when the enemy poured on mortar and small weapons fire, the remaining men went for cover in a trench when a grenade was tossed at them. Twenty-two-year-old Simanek heroically thrust himself onto the grenade, absorbing the explosion with his body and shielding the other marines from death or critical injury. Incredibly, he survived. Following months at a hospital, he was given his medal by President Dwight D. Eisenhower.

Unlike that of Simanek, who was just a few years older, Donnie's service record would reflect nothing outstanding or remarkable. After all, it was only weeks before his white fellow Michigan serviceman's selfless act that the last Negro unit had been disbanded. The American public expressed support of Truman's work in progress to integrate the military. While MacArthur had been reluctant to accept desegregated combat forces, the Project Clear social study found that integration raised morale among all the troops, but especially among black soldiers, and that it led to a better distribution of skills. Also noted in Project Clear was the observation that fewer race-related incidents took place within integrated troops than within still-segregated units. At the beginning and end of the day, the soldiers all put on and took off the same color of uniform. Nevertheless, the National Association for the Advancement of Colored People reported that black soldiers were more frequently subject to court martial, the trial process for alleged violations of military law, during the Korean conflict. Whether it was due to a lingering desire to test boundaries or lingering discrimination in the ranks, as his military career progressed, Donnie spent his share of time in the "pokey," as he called it. Like other Negroes in the service, the boy who had achieved little in Detroit joined the service at a time when proving himself would come at a greater cost than it would to others. A few rose to the task, like Captain Daniel "Chappie" James, Jr., with whom Donnie had a service branch in common. James flew a fighter jet on dangerous, unarmed reconnaissance missions behind enemy lines, which was a task reserved for the most skilled and trusted pilots. He became the air force's first black officer to command a fighter squadron. Similarly, Second Lieutenant Frank E. Peterson, Jr., the first black pilot in the marines, flew a total of sixty-four combat missions. And the navy's Jesse Brown was the first Negro aviator to die in combat when his plane was shot down.

Though Donnie's achievements were less spectacular, they were among his most legitimate claims of merit. In the strangest irony, some time between his disciplinary actions and the date he was discharged, Donnie became a military police officer. Clearly, the air force didn't know what it had on its hands. Like others on the police squad, he was given access to classified information and restricted areas. Donnie made a handsome, if unlikely, young officer when he put on his suit and sidearm. He learned to drive a truck as well, while overseas. Had he chosen to, he might have parlayed either one of his occupations into a long-time career. But the surroundings in Japan and mainland Korea, where he was later stationed, were not the most conducive to the development of a teenager. If guns and violence weren't a harmfully conditioning presence, there were distractions and temptation, the likes of which resembled nothing of those Joe and Myrtle had raised him to be accustomed to. Along with newly acquired skills, Donnie would carry demons from East Asia for the duration of his days, the kind that were more difficult to exorcise than he had probably been capable of imagining.

Of at least 600,000 Negroes who served in the armed forces

during Korea, an estimated 5,000 others perished in the conflict. Still, there was another heavy toll taken on the lives of a number who survived the war. It was a slower death than that inflicted by bullets or explosions, but it proved to be in many respects equally devastating. It was rumored that China's leadership used the drug heroin as a secret weapon of sorts to undermine the opponents of communism. Heroin was said to have been exported to Japan, throughout other parts of Asia, and into the United States. Chinese allegedly targeted American bases with the sleep-inducing narcotic, which was recreationally used by an indeterminate number of servicemen. Yet, if there was a drug-distributing attack strategy utilized by China during the war, there was little evidence to support it. Heroin was already widely available in large Asian cities, including Korea's capital, when the American soldiers arrived. And not an insignificant number of the enlisted were already familiar with the narcotic: It had begun infiltrating the States and incriminating itself in urban communities as early as the previous decade. As best anyone could tell, Donnie first got the urge to get high after he'd reached Asian soil. He started out by smoking. Hash. Marijuana. Opium. Heroin came last. Among his other adventures there was the experience of sex with prostitutes. The whores made themselves compatible with any serviceman who conveyed an interest. Donnie developed such an enjoyment of the willing women that he had himself photographed while receiving their pleasures. His drug habit was simultaneously captured for the camera during one or two encounters with naked Korean ladies. To be certain, none of the boys in the gang on his old block were fucking like this.

As the months passed, Joe and Myrtle adjusted to the idea that their son was a full-fledged member of the military. Joe and Myrtle ultimately decided that the experience might be a good one for him. Help teach him responsibility. Introduce him to manhood. They had no way of knowing what other introductions he was receiving. For that matter, they may have underestimated what he'd seen and done before he ever left for the service. Clairette, who had been so concerned that Myrtle be nearby when she gave birth to the grandboy, passed away before she could ever see him in his uniform; George would remarry twice before his own death. In any event, Donnie's family knew he was out of their hands. Fighting finally ended in Korea on July 27, 1953. South Korea gained about 1,500 square miles of land, and both sides agreed they would not increase their military strength. The United States spent an estimated $67 billion funding its efforts in the war. A million civilians were killed in South Korea. Damages to property were estimated at $1 billion. An exchange of close to 90,000 war prisoners was among the last steps in a process before peace negotiations. Donnie was issued an honorable discharge for his contributions. When he prepared to return home he was just seventeen.

Dope Fiend

He must certainly have been one of the few black writers in history to be avidly read by junkies, winos and prostitutes, who not only read his books on street corners and buses, but actually discussed them! I observed this myself. Unsurprisingly, he was a junkie, himself, but he had a flair for capturing and interpreting black street culture in all of its richness, excitement, danger and tragedy.

—Paul Lee, *Our-storian*

Joan heard a car slowing to a stop outside. At five years old, she was still becoming accustomed to the traditions of the Goines clan. It was Sunday morning. Myrtle carefully dressed her youngest daughter as they prepared to attend service at Sacred Heart. It seemed an ordinary morning to Myrtle as she looked the child over in the upstairs bedroom, but Joanie's attention remained fixed on who was in the vehicle on the ground below.

"Here comes Donnie, Momma!" she exclaimed.

Myrtle paid the child, who'd heard about but had no real memory of her brother, little attention.

"Oh, that can't be my Donnie. He's far away in another country," she said, distracted.

"Uh huh, yes it is."

Then suddenly a door opening took her mother's mind from its momentary preoccupation with little girls' church clothes.

"My boy is back! Thank you, Jesus!" Myrtle shouted, excitedly.

In the doorway stood a young, handsome soldier wearing his air force uniform. Donnie and Myrtle embraced tightly as tears rolled down their faces. It was classic Americana. Almost like a Norman Rockwell painting. Myrtle's only boy, who had run away from home, was a war veteran. He had traveled thousands of miles across the ocean, and Jesus had returned him to her safely. Surely, now things would be fine. There would be no more worrying about him wreaking havoc in the neighborhood or getting himself into trouble. Surely what would follow for Donnie would be a bright future. Nothing would turn Myrtle's boy around. The overjoyed mother couldn't see it at that time, as she wiped the tears from her face, but things were not to be nearly so simple. When she cried over Donnie the next time, it would be out of pain. It would be out of the anguished feeling that she was completely helpless in cushioning his reckless fall. When she next called on Jesus for Donnie, it would be to save her boy from complete destruction.

The days that followed Donnie's return home ran together rather quickly. He moved in with his parents and Joanie until he could get settled and readjust to civilian life. He and Joe remained distant, holding no open hostility, but speaking little to each other, even though they shared roles and responsibilities as men of the house. Still, they had little in common except that they were father and son. There was no outward hostility, but nothing in Joe's words or demeanor suggested Donnie had earned his father's respect by surviving for two years on his own. Joe mostly continued to concern himself with running the business, as had been his way for as long as Donnie could remember. He maintained hope that his son would take over the business. But by now, Donnie wanted no part of dry cleaning. As far as he was concerned, he had done enough time at Northside as a child to last him the rest of his days. To hell with the old man if he didn't recognize the value of Donnie's earlier work. After all, there was a world waiting. He was back on familiar turf. And there was still plenty to see and reacquaint himself with in the community that he remembered.

The Bookmobile would visit various neighborhoods every Monday and Wednesday. Onboard there were librarians who worked and saw to the needs of students who might not be able to make their way over to the nearby branch after school. Other young people found ways to hustle, as Donnie had begun to do before his enlistment. Peoples Bar on Hastings was a hangout for children hoping to make good with a little pocket change: They knew that their old man or another kid's old man would go in on the weekend and come out feeling no pain. Usually, an intoxicated dad or two could be counted on to distribute a few quarters. Or he might be so hampered that he would reach too deep in his pockets and pull them inside out, leaving all the change he had to bounce around in a free-for-all on the concrete. Other kids spent time as apprentices to the elder hustlers, observing how they went about creating a way for themselves. Pimps and prostitutes generally showed kindness to children, so the boys and girls might pick a favorite to assist now and then. When Michigan winters arrived, the prostitutes got crafty about how they could keep warm in the alleys and doorways by warming bricks. A dollar might be earned by a helper who kept bricks heated and maintained the haphazard platforms that kept the women from dirtying themselves by having to crouch down toward the warmth. Often, such young ones would go to a ten-cent store, pocket the money, and steal everything they could. Most of Donnie's peers were preparing for senior prom or graduation. Of course, such concerns were no longer relevant in his life.

Donnie set about looking for work. He never really cared for traditional employment. He had the mentality of a boss but only the resources of a job candidate. Something would have to give, though. He'd lived as a grown man since he had snuck his way into the military, so he was expected to continue living as a grown man. He began to pound the pavement. In time, his air force experience as a truck driver appeared to pay off. Donnie briefly found work behind the wheel again, but his lackadaisical attitude was ill-suited for the responsibility of transporting and delivering. For one thing, it required him to keep a schedule. Filling out travel logs and time slips and such was another discipline for him altogether. Donnie also tried employment on the assembly line of Pittsburgh Plate Glass. But it wasn't long again before he was back to spending his days shooting pool, smoking weed, and killing time with other similarly unambitious acquaintances. After catching hell from Joe or Myrtle, he'd be right back to square one again. But there was a major distraction from his job hunt, and it wasn't just a preoccupation with casual hobbies. Of all the things he had left behind in Korea, unfortunately, his habit was not one. Heroin, along with opium and cocaine, already had history in Detroit. The drug-user customer base numbered in the tens of thousands. In fact, the *Detroit Free Press,* a local daily paper, had reported a large presence of dope fiends in the city as early as 1912. When Donnie went out looking for action, he also looked for ways to feed his addiction. Drug pushers became gradually more prominent in the world of hustling. As demand for a good high increased, their willingness to supply corresponded. In parts of the city, narcotics were almost as readily available as over-the-counter cold medicine or cigarettes. Donnie wasted little time in making the appropriate connections to get what he needed.

Of course, the music was partly to blame.

Shoo be bop be bop

At least indirectly.

Doo be doo be ske be doo

Those bad-ass jazz cats were the coolest on the set. By now, their music could be heard everywhere. It was ridiculous to think that these musicians were all influenced by some kind of addiction, but by the same token, pushers jockeyed for unofficial celebrity endorsements. They offered free dope to the performers. At times, amazingly, the suppliers found out where touring musicians would stay overnight before the musicians ever got word. Jazz brothers served as walking billboards for whatever happened to be hip at the time. As a result, lots of fans got hooked, often confusing the talent and creative ability of those they revered with some kind of drug-induced brilliance that manifested itself in the sweetest sounds. It was one misleading, fucked-up fad. In truth, the musicians had spent plenty of sober hours honing their crafts. If they still carried those devastating tunes when they were high, it was because they were on autopilot. The legendary Charlie "Bird" Parker was a good example. A magnificent saxophonist, his beginnings resembled Donnie's in some striking ways. Parker dropped out of school, like Donnie, at age fifteen. And the musician had also answered the call of heroin when he was still traversing through adolescence. As he rose through the ranks as a top-flight artist, his addiction became a hindrance, as would the habit of his band mate, trumpeter Miles Davis, who played in Bird's quintet. Bird was idolized, nonetheless. It made little difference to his admirers that years of heroin and alcohol were helping to bring about his death. Who could know the numbers of others affected as destructively by the trend?

Though no one could be sure what kind of music was playing in Donnie's head, it was soon apparent that he had a problem. In fact, he probably didn't make much of an effort to hide it. The cravings and the urgency to use were unlike any that healthy young people could have experienced, save hunger and the need to use the restroom. Donnie's very blood had developed a dependency on the substance that held in its powdery components the powers to bring pleasure and pain. More than a few soldiers had become addicted to medications that numbed them to their physical discomforts. In civilian life, drug abuse became as normal to Donnie as waking up in the morning. As the weeks and months got behind him, his habit remained a companion. At some point, though, he recognized that the addiction was a destructive one. He approached his mother and Joanie, now an older child, with sincerity. Donnie believed he could kick his habit with just a little help and support. It wouldn't be a simple challenge, but he felt capable of meeting it. Donnie asked Myrtle and Joanie to lock him in his bedroom. He anticipated how the withdrawal symptoms might cause him to react. They would have to promise, Donnie told them, that no matter how he persisted— ranting, raving, crying or pleading—not to let him out until he had completely rid his body of reliance on the smack that he pumped through his system. Myrtle had never imagined that she would be frightened of her special boy. But the reality of the screams and curses that eventually came from behind the locked door were chilling. Myrtle and Joanie could only listen. If there had been any temptation to free him from his self-imposed solitary confinement, his aggressive reactions to being suddenly without drugs at his disposal removed them.

"Open this goddamn door!"

Donnie was like a man possessed. And this was exorcism.

"Let me live my own life!" he screamed. "Aaaaah! Goddammit! Mind your own damned business!"

Under ordinary circumstances he never spoke to his mother or baby sister this way. Now, he was a person they didn't recognize. Intense chills, nausea, and cramps could leave a junkie with feelings of sickness that no visit to the pharmacy would be able to cure. It was simply more of a monster than Donnie could handle. Ultimately, he escaped from his prison, and did so repeatedly after any number of similar attempts. He might be reduced to groveling like a pitiful child one day, asking *"Please,* Mama," or muster all his might and fury to break the door down the next. Whether he had to beg and plead, tear loose hinges, or tunnel through the floor to the ground outside, he was determined to get a fix. Once he had found his medicine, he returned home content, as if he had not felt near the verge of death just a few hours earlier. His efforts were honest ones; his opponent more worthy than he'd imagined. Myrtle and Joanie kept trying, despite the terror it brought them. After all, they loved Donnie.

Not completely aware of the vice her brother struggled against, Marie was contending with other stress. She had married at seventeen, while still a student at Cass Technical High School in 1951. Myrtle and Joe were against it, but she raised such hell that they finally relented and gave their consent. Charles Glover had grown up in the neighborhood along with Marie and Donnie. He was employed at the post office and struck Marie as a pretty stable young man. At nineteen, he decided he was ready to be a husband. Not long afterward, the couple began having children. Marie's first baby died, but in all, there would be three boys: Charles Jr., Robert, and Sammy. In time, Marie began to see another side of her young husband. Charles was a gambler, and she came to view their marriage as a mistake. He became abusive toward Marie. Charles took to manhandling, not difficult to manage with a lady of Marie's weight and size. She was wholly unaccustomed to anything besides peace, refuge, and formal table settings in a home. Now, with not only herself, but also little ones to consider, she had to review her options carefully. She learned to fight back. Marie had gotten around a bit after all, it appeared. One time she opened up Charles's head with a fireplace poker. She borrowed a page from the days of slavery resistance and crushed bits of glass into her husband's food. Occasionally, she would add a laxative to the recipe. Marriage became psychological warfare. Then Donnie came to mind. Knowing that he was around gave Marie relief from her sense of helplessness. After getting the word from her, Donnie rounded up a few of his partners and they paid Charles a visit. The confrontation made its point, but the marriage would not last.

Before she was twenty, Marie became a dancer for the Harlem Globetrotters. Neither well-traveled nor from New York, the athletes, whose collective name was conceived as a marketing gimmick, had at one time been regarded one of the best basketball teams in the world. During the course of her road trips, Marie would encounter a player who briefly appeared on the Globetrotters roster before signing professionally with the Philadelphia Warriors. At seven feet and one inch tall, Wilt Chamberlain was destined for greatness. He had attracted attention since his days as a high-school athlete on the East Coast. Chamberlain and the eldest Goines daughter began dating. At barely sixty vertical inches, Marie chuckled when she thought of the fact that she was the height of "Wilt the Stilt's" belt buckle, which suited him just fine. The high-scoring center was only one of several celebrities Marie met during her travels. She had also become a "pony girl," or backup dancer, for Cab Calloway. While Marie toured the nation with the different troupes, she observed a society in the process of change. There had been no reported lynchings since 1951, but in

1955, three Negroes fell victim to the familiar southern evil. One was fourteen-year-old Chicagoan Emmett Louis Till.

The boy had badgered Mamie Till Bradley to allow him to visit family in the town of Money, Mississippi, as they had paid him a visit in Illinois. One day during his trip in late August, Emmett and about eight of his cousins took his uncle's old Ford to a nearby market in Money, where they had what proved to be a fateful encounter with the pretty white clerk, Carolyn Bryant. Big-talking Emmett was urged to make a pass at her. So, choosing not to back down, the city slicker went inside, where he hugged the woman's waist and squeezed her hand, whistling on his way out. Bryant claimed later that he said "Bye, baby," as his companions rushed him away, fearful that he had gone much too far.

Days later, outraged men, including Bryant's husband, showed up with pistols at the home of Emmett's uncle, Mose Wright, about 2 A.M. In short order, they snatched the boy outside and disappeared with him. His body, nude, brutalized, and decomposing, was later discovered by another teenager while he was fishing in the Tallahatchie River. It appeared that Emmett had been put through a hellish torture: A seventy-five-pound cotton gin fan was fastened to his neck with barbed wire, his skull was partially crushed, and an eye was missing. Hundreds of news reporters arrived at the rural courthouse where two white men were put on trial for taking a black life. The judge refused to let the store clerk give her testimony, believing that it would inflame the jury, though she had already done plenty of talking about what had occurred. Neither Bryant's husband, nor his half-brother, took to the witness stand. None of Emmett's young cousins who'd been at the market would testify, either. One of the boys who had accompanied Emmett to Mississippi was prevented from returning, for fear that his safety might be at stake. At sixty-four, Mose Wright, however, took perhaps the boldest step of anyone toward gaining justice for his nephew. It was an unwritten rule that black folks didn't testify against whites in court, but the old man was asked to identify the men he had watched helplessly dragging Emmett off into the darkness of the early morning. Wright stood and pointed at the codefendants, saying "There he." In the broken

English that it was delivered, the statement was no less dramatic and should have been no less damning. But an all-white jury deliberated for just over an hour, and a juror arrogantly confided in one reporter that it had only taken this long because they stopped for a soda break. The men were found not guilty of both the murder and the more obvious charge of kidnapping. Public outcry rejecting the verdict provided momentum for what eventually became an era dedicated to challenging the existing social system. "The life of a Negro in Mississippi," declared one foreign newspaper, "is not worth a whistle." Mamie Till Bradley became a lecturer, referring to her son as a "little nobody who shook up the world."

Demonstrations had little immediate effect on justice in Mississippi. Mose Wright left the state to be with his Chicago family, while the men who killed his nephew stayed behind to brag about their crime. The pair received $4,000 from a publication in exchange for telling their story: They claimed they had abducted Emmett and brutalized him to frighten the child, which they had acknowledged during the trial. But when the boy showed he was too proud to beg for mercy or apologize, they said, they had little choice but to murder him. The racists said Till was shot in the head and then they threw him in the river after he was given one last chance to deny believing his humanity equaled that of a Caucasian yet refused it. J. W. Milam seemed as if his only regret in the child's killing was that Emmett hadn't known better, when he was quoted as saying: "What else could we do? He was hopeless. He thought he was as good as any white man. I'm no bully. I never hurt a nigger in my life. I like niggers—in their place. I know how to work 'em. But I just decided it was time a few people got put on notice."

Marie found that in Alabama, where she also performed, there was a different type of notice being given. Months after the Till case, the city's capital of Montgomery found itself crippled significantly. In December 1955, 42,000 Negro residents began a year-long boycott of the public transportation system. Ordinance called for black passengers to sit in the rear, gradually decreasing their allotted space as more white passengers boarded. The previous year, on May 17, the U.S. Supreme Court ruled that separate-but-unequal facilities in education were unconstitutional. Five different cases that had challenged the legality of segregation in schools had originated in South Carolina, Virginia, Kansas, Delaware, and the District of Columbia. *Oliver Brown et al.* v. *Board of Education* became the landmark decision that decried the separation of white and black children in public schools. Oliver Brown had tried to send his eight-year-old daughter to an all-white elementary school located just a short distance from her home in Topeka, Kansas. The court ruled unanimously that "separate educational facilities are inherently unequal." Discrimination through the school system had a detrimental effect on black youth, the court decided. Separate school facilities created feelings of inferiority related to their standing in the community. Substandard buildings and accommodations, entirely apart from the inability to go to school with white children, might have been just as damaging to their self-esteem.

For whatever reason, though, the Montgomery power structure viewed bigotry on the bus as a whole unrelated category. Boycott organizers distributed approximately 52,000 fliers asking blacks to find alternatives to public transportation. Armed with shotguns, police roamed the streets seeking any intimidators who forced other blacks off the city vehicles. Later, the cops threatened to arrest taxi drivers who gave discount rates to black passengers. Aside from cabs and moving about by foot, former bus riders joined car pools, but they caught similar hell in attempting to get where they wanted to go. Police harassed the drivers, citing them for traveling too fast or too slowly. It wouldn't have taken a discerning person to recognize that Montgomery's leadership was feeling economic pressure. The segment of the population it had alternately disregarded and exploited was taking away its power. By the end of the demonstration another court ruling outlawed segregated seating in public transportation. The victory, however, had not come without its casualties. Along with the legal intimidation they faced from police, members of the black community were given hell by the White Citizens Council. Believing that there were outside forces influencing the protest, the racists turned their attention toward boycott leaders. Other groups went as far as setting off bombs at black homes and churches. It was a contradictory and confusing message to suggest that the presence of Negroes on Montgomery's buses was less desirable than that of whites but to simultaneously terrorize Negroes for their refusal to ride those very same buses.

Even in the Baughs' hometown of Little Rock, where Marie had family roots, there was resistance and upheaval. President Eisenhower ordered 1,000 military paratroopers to Arkansas to protect children who were only a few years younger than the eldest Goines child at the time. Whites had become rabidly violent after efforts got underway to integrate Central High School, pursuant to the Brown decision. Activist Daisy Bates helped coordinate the admission of the first group of nine black students, who became known as the Little Rock Nine. The governor made his pro-segregation feelings known, while other racists urged white children to work hard at driving their new classmates into submission. A sampling of newspaper headlines told the story of the Nine's struggle and the community's resistance to the idea of having them walk the same halls white children walked: "Guard platoon sent to school after threats of bombing"; "Another racial clash reported at Central High"; "Dynamite found at CHS . . ."; "Another bomb scare disrupts CHS routine . . ."; "CHS plagued by more bomb scares"; "New bomb scare at Central High proves false"; "Another bomb tossed at LC Bates' house"; "Negro parents take insults, pray for children's safety." The students were routinely shoved down stairs, kicked, tripped, threatened, and attacked with ink on their clothes, books, lockers, and seats. One of the children wrote in her diary about a day she experienced in February: "I got hit across the back with a tennis racquet. I managed to smile and say, 'Thank you.' Andy said, 'What did you say, nigger?' I repeated, 'Thank you very much.' I spit up blood in the restroom." The governor had called in the National Guard to prevent the Nine from entering the building to begin with. When he was compelled—but only by a court order—to remove the guardsmen, a hysterical, raging mob defied police and forced their removal from the school. The troops Eisenhower ordered would remain on guard for the rest of the school year after the Nine returned. The governor ultimately closed Central High and other public buildings in Little Rock, saying he refused to open the schools as integrated institutions. He became a regional hero, as southerners attempted to let it be known that they were not prepared for a new way of life that included sitting next to Negroes on buses, in classrooms or elsewhere. Not until 1960 were the schools forced to reopen.

By the time Marie returned to the relative peace of Detroit, she was prepared to settle. She went back to reside with the family at the Goines home. It didn't take long for her to realize that things had changed considerably where the stability of her siblings was concerned. Even as she had traveled the country, witnessing various forms of failure, success, and survival in cities all over the map, she had seen nothing like the full-blown addiction of a real-life junkie. The boy who called her "Wee Wee" had grown up but into someone possessed by something she didn't truly understand. Smack. It had been given this, among other nicknames, because of the heroin addict's habit of smacking his or her arm in order to find a vein where it could be injected. The whole filthy notion was about as far from Marie's experience as traveling to the moon, which astronauts had only recently achieved. Donnie had become a captive, and she could find no hope of freeing her brother. Part of him would have had to acknowledge that he wanted no taste of this freedom anyway. Freedom from such a bittersweet high would mean a sober reality. A sober reality would mean a cold, hard look at the stress and challenges of his readjustment to the existence he'd left behind in his late childhood. Whatever the source of his anxiety or pain, whatever the source of his irritation, getting high was a form of relief. Searching for a job, meeting his parents' expectations, even brushing his teeth or washing his ass—it could all wait, said the all-mighty, all-soothing needle. Every little thing would be just fine.

The cost of a house in Detroit averaged about $13,000 in 1956. Young folks like Donnie and Marie had become eager to work and start families. There had been a demand for new homes, and they were built at a rate never to be matched in the metropolitan area. The typical new house was about 1,300 square feet and had three bedrooms. Picture windows could be found in the living areas, and garbage disposals became standard kitchen features. Symbolic of its economic blessings, the metropolis had its share of mansions. Henry Ford's and that of Lawrence P. Fisher, one of the founding brothers in the Fisher Body Company, were both built at a cost of $2.5 million. And David Whitney, a lumber baron, had a gated, palatial estate near downtown. Constructed in 1894, it remained proudly facing Woodward Avenue. Detroit was proving a good place to succeed, and it was about time for the next generation of Goines adults to partake in that success. But Marie had been unable to help her brother, as he had helped her. She had found herself just as relegated to the sidelines of his junkie life as the rest of the family. Often, they could do little more than wonder in amazement. Like the day when she happened to intercept the package of weed that had been sent to Donnie in the mail. Naïve as she was, she didn't even recognize the contents of the delivery as anything illegal. If there was one thing she and his other relatives could count on gaining from Donnie, though, it was awareness of what was going on in the outside world. In the world from which they had long sheltered themselves when they were having formal dinners with desperation and despair on the opposite side of the door. Now, smack was pushing Donnie toward it.

Fiend.

By the time he was only twenty-four, Donnie had accepted the notion behind the word. Where drugs were concerned, he couldn't deny himself. Smack would be his companion for life. He didn't control the habit; the habit controlled him. Without looking into professional help or treatment that would restrict his freedom, he determined to at least do good by making an example of himself. One evening as he prepared to fix, he got the idea to call Joanie in for a demonstration. Still just a child, her innocence exceeded even that of prissy Marie. She was growing up a Goines during the time when Joe and Myrtle were well settled and had not been a witness to the way they once drank whiskey, partied, and socialized. Now they worked during the day and went to bed early. All Joanie knew was that her brother, the same nice young man who had presented her with the red silk kimono he brought back from overseas when she was small, had developed a serious problem. The twelve-year-old was wide-eyed as Donnie began the process of self-medication.

"Don't you ever let me catch you doing this, Poopty," her brother said, as he cooked the powdery, white substance. Joanie watched, mesmerized as he held a burning match beneath the metal spoon, turning the powder into a clear liquid. This would be a lesson she could never forget. Donnie was saying "I love you" through a strange ritual of self-sacrifice. It would eventually kill him anyway, he figured, so he might as well make it count for something. Joanie tried to look at the floor.

"Watch, Poopty," Donnie told her. The gentleness in his voice might have sent a chill down her neck, except that she knew he cared for her. So why was he making her watch such a strange thing? Joanie's eyes didn't wander. They took in the full scene, as Donnie pushed the needle through his pale flesh. Suddenly sleepy, he raised his head toward his baby sister one last time before drifting off. "Poopty . . ." he started. "I promise . . . if you ever get this monkey on your back, I'll kill you."

It was a more effective presentation than she would ever receive in school. Contradictory as Donnie's message was—to insist that she heed his words rather than his actions—it penetrated her young consciousness. If this was the demon that so completely controlled her brother, she wanted no part of it. Self-injection was not a sight that came comforting to Joanie. Nor did the thought of chills and nausea, cramps, or pissing on herself when side effects from the drug, or withdrawal reactions, seized control of her bladder. Through her formative years, she would watch Donnie shoot up numerous times. He'd go in search of a scarf, a string, a stocking, anything he could find to tie around his arm, and then look for a juicy vein. Next, he would use a homemade syringe, fashioned out of an eyedropper and a discarded needle, which was easily obtained from Myrtle's insulin tubes. He attached the needles to the tip of the dropper and would proceed to retreat from reality. Joanie would watch, disgusted, as blood seeped into the tube, blending with the heroin, and Donnie would pump the concoction back into his arm.

His handsome face would contort from the pain of the injection, then relax as he drifted toward the oblivious high he sought to achieve. It was a lot for a young girl to take in, to say the least. Ulti- mately, however, it served its purpose. Joanie may not have decided what she wanted to be when she grew up, but at least one thing be- came clear: She never wanted to be a dope fiend.

Cash and Bitches

*"You better damn well bet I'm sure," Tiny stated. "We been watchin'
that numbers house for three weeks now, and I'm sure we can crack
it . . ."*

*. . . Buddy answered sharply, then added, "but this ain't no toy,
man. These people play for keeps. If we kick this joint over, we goin'
have to play it mighty cool after that, 'cause they sure in the fuck
ain't 'bout to forget us."*

*"Aw, man," Tiny said, "let's worry about skinning that cat when
we get to it. For now, we got to knock the fuckin' joint off. After that,
then we'll worry 'bout spendin' the cash."*

—*Daddy Cool*, Donald Goines

It became known as the "bitch slap." And there was an art to it. A
good number of street pimps employed the technique, yet fewer
could truly claim they had become masters. While inflicting the recipient with some measure of pain was always the result, it wasn't
necessarily the main goal. This form of assault, when committed
by a pimp on a prostitute, was mainly for effect. It was a display of
dominance, both to the recipient and any observers. A pimp had to
have it known at all times that he was in charge of his shit. No confusion. The slap was best delivered at a slightly downward angle,
from a height with the palm about eye level. It was ideally given
from a position with the arm bent close to ninety degrees and extended directly to the side. A quick, stinging bitch slap made just
the right sound to get one's point across. If a whore could hear the
noise of her flesh being battered, she tended to take the reprimand
more seriously. It wasn't required, or always possible, that she be

knocked to the ground; considering differences in size and strength, however, putting a woman on the floor was like a bonus. When other stablemates, or "wives-in-law," were witnesses to such discipline, they usually took heed. A talented pimp knew how to say the words "You could be next," without ever opening his mouth. It was about style and finesse.

Physical discipline could be given for various reasons. A prostitute whose money was short could be a good candidate. If she brought her man less than what was expected of her, she was not on her job. Selling ass was no half-ass form of work. Another offense that could get a girl bitch-slapped was excess lip. No self-respecting pimp would abide a sassy-ass woman who didn't know when to shut the fuck up. Then there was theft. A woman who stole money from her pimp committed the ultimate betrayal. After all, he took care of her, provided her with a bed to sleep in and pretty clothes to wear. Smart pimps, like any good businessmen, would reward them for their performance now and then, too. All the girls had to do was look good, which was what most women tried to do anyway, and know how to spread their legs. They could ask for money when they needed it. "Daddy" was the pimp's title for more reasons than one. By the same token, a bitch knew when a nigger was inexperienced. A nigger who couldn't slap properly was better off giving icy stares and menacing glances to keep his women in line. Otherwise, he might be tested more frequently than was appropriate for any respectable pimp. Even a loud and brash talker could convincingly suggest what fury he was capable of demonstrating if his bitch didn't know how to act. But the worst thing he could ever allow was for a prostitute to begin treating him like one of her tricks. That could happen subtly enough that he'd be taken without even realizing it, if he wasn't careful.

Donnie would have none of that, of course. He entered the pimping profession with serious intent. To hell with a job. He had always been best suited for self-employment, anyway. So why not make a living on his own terms? The odds seemed as good as any. Where he had suffered for his complexion as a boy, high yellow was more fashionable now. With the increasing knowledge that women found him attractive, his confidence that he could do what other woman-handlers in the city had done for years and years only grew. He had a charm about him, and at five feet eight, with a medium build, he was easy on the eyes. Where he was once self-conscious about his physical appearance, now he used it to his advantage. He developed his rap, that special knack for telling the sisters what they wanted to hear. If a brother had the look but could do nothing but stumble over his own tongue, he wasn't about to make much of a lasting impression. And if he were shy, there would be little reason for a woman to think he was worth choosing as a pimp daddy. An air of confidence was as vital as air for inhalation. Donnie had golden brownish hair and eyes that most ladies found exotically attractive. They appeared to change color with his moods: a mellow blue when he was happy, greenish when he became excited, and a fiery brown with hints of gold when he was enraged. Through them he watched vulnerable prey and began to scope out recruits for his fledgling stable. Donnie became a master at picking up and handling women. They loved him and flocked to him like sheep being herded.

Before long, he was able to bring them under his control, ruling with an iron hand. He was reminded of the Korean prostitutes he'd enjoyed as a teenager. They had been young, tender to the touch, and eager to please. He got a bit of his money together and began to dress the part. He planned to outdo Goldfinger, Silky Slim, and other better-known Detroit pimps who came before him. Preferring suit colors like aqua and sky blue, Donnie began to gain a profile. And since like hustlers thought with like minds, it wasn't surprising when he began running around with a few fellow outlaws. True partners in crime, like Walter, for example. Donnie and Walter went way back, having lived as roommates on a few different occasions. Like Donnie, Walter had served in Korea, though he was a few years older and had gone to the army before his friend enlisted in the air force. Later on, Walter and Donnie shared an apartment over a bakery on Dexter Avenue. Walter had worked for Dodge, but he took to hustling because he figured it would pay greater dividends. Yet, during their dry spells the two men found themselves with hunger and no way of feeding it. The pair would go downstairs and show all the charm and manners their parents taught them, in order to talk the store's employees out of occasional free cakes and pastries. Although they were all for one and one for all at times like these, if his wallet was full, Walter had to be watchful around his buddy, or it might come up missing. He knew Donnie had a "jones," as habits were called in those days; Walter just didn't want to get in the routine of financing it. At one point, they took on weed-selling as a means of profit. Visitors would stop by their place asking for one or the other, hoping to make a buy. Walter had created his own special system for stocking packets of marijuana. He removed from their narrow, open slots the wooden sticks that served as handles for window shades. Then he carefully folded the weed and stuffed as much of it as he could fit from one end of the shades to the other. It was a crafty way of hiding evidence if the apartment was ever raided. But the whores came along and made it an entirely different game.

As their ventures began generating income, Donnie and his partners would make a grand show of shopping downtown for expensive shoes and designer clothing. One day when they were out on one of their excursions near the Fox Theatre, during the era when it held the wildly popular "Motortown Revue" performances, a few of them nearly stopped traffic out on busy Woodward Avenue. They had been mistaken for the Temptations. With cash, a stable of bitches, and attention from admiring strangers, who needed a job? Hell, Joe had slaved in a cleaning plant in order to afford everything he bought the family. As Donnie shuffled between dope dens, whorehouses, and other places of ill repute, however, it seemed to matter little to him, if at all, that, by contrast, he had become nothing more than a common criminal.

Bumper tag became the sport of choice. Late at night, Donnie and his buddies would fly their vehicles full-speed down Detroit freeways, metal-tapping the rear of each other's stylish rides, often with girls standing, dangerously, through the open roofs. In many ways Donnie's rebellious years symbolized the prime of his life. The 1950s and '60s were not a good time for black men in America, if ever there was such a thing, yet he was taking destiny into his own hands with complete fearlessness and reckless abandon. "Turning out" women, as the process of recruiting them into the life of prostitution was called, became a meal ticket.

Not even fatherhood could distract him from his work and mission. Alfonso, Donnie's first American-born seed, had been conceived with a woman named Virginia Chambers. Donnie lived with her in the Hamtramck area for a time, right next to a funeral casket company. But the domestic setup didn't particularly suit him. He moved on. Thelma Howard gave birth to Anthony, little Donald, and Christopher between 1960 and 1965. Still, Donnie was ill-prepared and ill-equipped to be anybody's parent. He confessed to Joanie and Marie that he had, in fact, left a child over in Asia. That boy or girl would be forever disconnected, for better or worse, from his legacy, they all presumed. If Donnie knew it, he never even shared the baby's name.

Donnie had genuinely achieved status in his family as the black sheep with a fair complexion. He became something they saw as truly outrageous. Myrtle didn't know what to do with her boy. Joanie found him embarrassing at times. Marie had witnessed his pimp antics once when she was at home and never would forget it. She peered down the street after hearing a commotion, and there Donnie stood, out on a corner in the middle of the day. He was loudly cursing and chastising a young prostitute as the girl listened timidly, cowering in his presence.

"What are you doing?" Marie yelled at her brother as she rushed outside and up the block. "Don't you talk to her like that!"

Suddenly the prostitute's demeanor changed to one of aggression.

"Who the fuck are you?" the girl yelled at Marie. "You better get out my man's face!"

In an instant, the prostitute was on the ground, the victim of a skillfully placed bitch slap. Donnie had struck her for speaking disrespectfully to his sister, the same sister who was scolding him for mistreating women. Joe was typically stoic and detached about the way his son carried on, except for one occasion when one of

Donnie's less attractive stable members dared to show up at the Goineses' front door. Large and dark brown, she was the antithesis of what the old man considered attractive. "Booga Bear" might have been the term used by less-sensitive folks who described her physically. But Booga Bears needed love, too, so Donnie put her to work like the rest. The woman was unlucky enough to have Joe as her greeter when she stopped by the house in search of Donnie on that particular day. She might have found him if Joe had not taken one look at her, slammed the door, and walked away.

Business had remained good for Joe Goines. Now well into his sixties, he had enjoyed the fruits of his labor and dedication. Dry cleaning had proved itself a worthy venture. He and Myrtle had been able to provide well for two children and would see that Joanie be given all she required until she left home. It was only a matter of time, after all, before she would marry and begin her own family. Joan and both her older siblings could truly say they had never wanted for anything material. For them to have had a need that went unmet could have only meant there had not truly been a need. In those later years, Joe began to find his own special ways to unwind at home. He had become a fan of Ray Charles, the blind pianist who was helping to develop rhythm and blues with his soulful performing and broad, expressive vocal and instrumental range. It was odd that Joe would take to the sounds of a performer who was laying the groundwork for rock and roll, but it turned out to be a musical release of sorts. Every so often, Joe would put on his ceremonial feathers and headdress. He called himself the "big chief." As he enjoyed the pride of such moments, he would turn on the stereo, and Charles would sing "Hit the Road, Jack," his playful and infectious hit about a contentious relationship. Nothing in the tune appeared to resemble Joe's life or his marriage to Myrtle. It might have been his strange, sacred way of communicating with his Native American ancestors. Or it might have been the alcohol accompanying the music. Either way, he was left alone. It was Joe's time to spend in whatever way that he chose to enjoy it. When time came to open the store and go back behind the counter at work, just like the sunrise, he was there. Donnie's work, on the other hand, generally started after dark. He worked the streets diligently, establishing revenue sources wherever he could.

Having returned home with Marie and her clan, while his mom's new husband continued a military bid, young Charles Joseph Glover frequently found himself in his uncle Donnie's company, and on the receiving end of unsolicited tutoring. Donnie wanted to school his nephew in the ways of the world so he wouldn't grow up to be a square. As it was, nobody in the neighborhood bothered Charles or any of the family members, out of respect for the man who they felt would repay any evil in kind. Still, Donnie wanted to prevent the kid from becoming soft. And left up to Marie, Donnie figured, the result was inevitable. So on one occasion, he and a partner decided to take Charles on a little field trip to a whorehouse on the east side near downtown. After taking him inside and attempting to persuade him into God-knows-what, they recognized that the boy was nowhere near capable of withstanding such pressure. Charles bolted, frightened, and got away from there. He could hardly wait to tell on Donnie when he saw his mother. But the price of his nervousness would be paid for some time to come. Childishly, they nicknamed him "Faggot Joey." After all, he had literally run away from pussy—and grown-woman pussy, at that. It was unheard of, and terribly laughable, in the pimping game.

Charles often saw his uncle after he got out of school. The mood he encountered one memorable time was noticeably pensive. He sat across from his uncle, eyeing him curiously. Draped in one of the fine European suits Charles's dad had sent from abroad, Donnie was the picture of concentration, his fist glued to his chin.

"What's wrong?" Charles asked.

"Shut up!" Donnie snapped. He fidgeted and twisted about in his seat. Someplace in the distance, Charles could hear pounding and muffled noises.

"What's that?"

"Shut up!" his uncle repeated. "You ask too many damn questions!" Donnie returned to his concentration. Shortly thereafter, Myrtle entered the room. Immediately, she detected tension.

"What are you doing?" she asked suspiciously.

"I'm thinkin'!" he sniped again. She left the room. In the background, Charles could still hear the pounding.

"What *is* that?" he nagged at his uncle.

"I told you to shut up!" Donnie paused. "You better keep your damn mouth shut if I tell you this." Charles listened. "We got this nigger tied up in the trunk . . ." As soon as Donnie began, it made sense; his uncle was crazy, Charles decided. That's all. Crazy. No other explanation. Like Joanie before him, Charles had been forced to witness the shooting up, Donnie's needle-injection demonstration. After several years, he was still watchful, in his perverse way, when it came to the children. Charles had also observed with interest Donnie's outrageous sky-blue suit and other pimp-wear. Soon-to-be film characters, like the ignorant and buffoonish 1970s pimp "Dolemite," with his kung fu–kicking prostitutes, were only pretenders to the style and life Donnie actually portrayed on the streets of Detroit. His nephew had witnessed the double-duty shoplifting missions that Donnie took his whores on at local grocery stores. Donnie and his bitches had shocked the sheltered boy as he sat out in the car. His uncle would go into the market wearing oversized coats that held secret compartments sewn into the lining. The girls might put a few items into a grocery basket—it wasn't exactly the kind of work they'd signed up for, but they took direction—then they'd all get in the checkout line. Standing behind them, Donnie whistled and glanced around as if lost for the moment in his own thoughts. He played the role of casual customer to the hilt. They'd pay for the few items presented to the cashier and walk out innocently to the parking lot. Victoriously, Donnie would open the trunk before snatching out an alarming number of steaks and packages of meat from his coat's lining. The food had been carefully concealed between the fabric of his outerwear and the shape of his inconspicuous frame.

"That's boosting!" he would proudly brag to his nephew. "I could teach you that, but you don't wanna know nothin' 'bout it!" Charles had also marveled at Uncle Donnie's sense of humor. His favorite show was *Bewitched*. He often sat with Charles and watched the antics of the sitcom's main character, Samantha, toward her mild-mannered husband Darrin, who was portrayed by eventual Michigan transplant Dick York.

"He's a punk!" Donnie would say, almost talking to the television.

"It's a TV show," Charles matter-of-factly explained.

"Aw man, he's a punk! He lets her walk all over him! He's a punk!" The rules of pimpology would probably not have applied to Darrin and Samantha's marriage anyway, but the mind-set, to Donnie, was all the same.

Charles reasoned with the macho pimp: "It's a *TV show*." Donnie enjoyed smoking reefer while he watched the program. Joan had a canary, whose cage sat next to Donnie's favorite chair in the living room. The bird would sing and whistle happily: *"Whrr-whrr-whrr, whrr-whrrr."* Donnie got a kick out of blowing reefer smoke into the cage. He'd take a puff, lean toward the bird, then exhale. Charles watched as the cheerful house pet received a contact high. This particular time, Donnie was feeling more devilish than usual.

"Watch this, Joey," he told Charles as he grinned at the bird. Donnie began his ritual: puff, lean, blow. He began to focus on the bird during *Bewitched* commercials. Puff, lean, blow. As if bewildered, now the bird chirped inconsistently.

"Whrr . . ."

After a while, Charles noticed that the bird was silent. He and Donnie got up, looked into the cage and saw it frozen on its perch. Donnie thumped the cage, and the poor thing fell over dead. Obviously, Joanie was at loss for laughter when she returned home from her job. Donnie got an earful like his sister had given him on only rare occasions. He responded in his usual sensitive fashion, saying that it was "just a bird."

Yep, crazy, Charles thought. That about summed it up. He listened to his uncle's dilemma concerning the man trapped outside in the car.

"I'm tryin' to decide whether we're gonna kill 'im or drop 'im off naked beside the road somewhere." He pondered the options the way a stockbroker would ponder an investment. Charles didn't bother to seek details about what transgression the poor fool at his uncle's mercy had committed. The fourteen-year-old reversed roles with his uncle, feeling that Donnie obviously needed a rational voice to help balance his thinking.

"You don't wanna kill him," Charles said, as if he'd made the decision at least a hundred times before. "Don't kill him."

Donnie sighed.

"Yeah. You're right. I don't need no murder case right now."

Charles never heard any more. Once he saw that Donnie agreed with his recommendation there was little left to say. But safest wagers would have had it that a naked man somewhere was left to find his way home after sundown. Donnie knew he could accomplish plenty on reputation alone. If he was respected as the bad ass he portrayed himself to be, there would be little need for him to work at supporting the image. Conserving energy and maximizing resources were just as important in the streets as anywhere. Advertising took on a slightly different form, though. Word of mouth could be more effective than any business card. Even so, Donnie never set out in search of trouble. He attempted to make it known, though, that any motherfucker who chose to test him would have a challenge on his or her hands. A little intimidation could go a long way.

At some point, Donnie decided he would take his pimp show on the road. With girls in tow, he left Detroit for the first time since his return from the air force. Donnie traveled out of state, heading westward in search of new trick money in places where he felt there'd be a demand. As personal experience had taught him, military personnel in need could be reliable customers. Donnie learned about a base in Kansas, where there would likely be men who were willing to part with their money for a piece of quality ass. He set up in the area for a while, until he drew the attention of local authorities. Not only that, but he managed to gain notice from the FBI, which opened a file on Donnie for what was peculiarly called "white slavery," that is, transporting prostitutes across state lines. The last thing he needed was a federal charge, which could mess up not only his game, but his prospects for running it. Fucking with a stiff federal sentence would obviously prohibit the money-making empire he envisioned himself in the process of building. Aware of the risks, when things heated up and his prospects changed, he went back in the direction of home. In Flint, about ninety minutes north of Detroit, he set up again. But it wasn't long before the movements of the stranger in town caught up with him once more. Cops didn't leave Donnie much room to breathe. No later than 1959, he was on Detroit soil once more. Now, however, Donnie was prepared to explore new ways to make a gain. There were surely quicker and simpler ways to get paid, without having to keep track of women. The money he spent on overhead, such as clothing and places to stay, could be direct-deposited into his pockets. Donnie's next major move would be designed to produce quicker and simpler dividends.

Numbers had a legacy and complexity that separated it from every other hustle in the ghetto. Its presence among the masses was far-reaching in both appeal and scope. Even many of the otherwise law-abiding citizens of black communities would occasionally "play the numbers" in hopes that their wagers would put them ahead enough to buy a new piece of furniture or maybe get ahead on the coming month's rent. Called "policy" around certain parts, like Chicago, the numbers game was the most carefully organized lottery system ever established by non-state, self-appointed authorities. It was said to have been brought over from the Caribbean by Afro-West Indians, who took and placed bets in barbershops and other small establishments that served as front stations for the lottery. Cities like Harlem, which attracted large numbers of immigrants, incorporated numbers into their subcultures as the newcomers learned of the affordability and simplicity of participating. Policy houses, where bets were taken and where the winners collected, were located on numerous blocks of northern cities. The winning numbers were chosen through various methods. New York used an already-established form of gambling as the source of its underground wage making: horse races. The numbers of the top three horses for each day served as the winning combination for bettors in Harlem. During another stage of the racket's evolution, the last three digits of the New York Stock Exchange's total trade volume was used to determine payout. Chicago had The Wheel, a roulette-style device that functioned as the proverbial magic lamp for numbers participants. Each day, players and policy organizers gathered at the selected location, perhaps a basement apartment or similar discreet place, and the wheel was spun before an anxious, enthusiastic—and usually packed—house. Though farther away in proximity from Harlem, Detroit numbers also went the way of the horse races in determining winners and losers.

What every city had in common was a basic structure, from bottom to top, of the players, ticket takers, operators, and financers involved with policy operation. Ticket takers, called "numbers runners," made their rounds to homes, street corners, shoeshine stands, soda shops, anyplace in the neighborhood where black folks gathered. The runners represented the first phase of monetary exchange, accepting bets that ranged from pennies to considerably larger amounts. Not uncommonly, these were teenagers who proved themselves responsible in keeping the dictates of the code. They began the process of recycling the healthy cash pool that constantly flowed from the pockets and purses of lower-income hopefuls into the hands of bank-rolling gangsters or benevolent hustlers—who were sometimes one and the same—and then back into the ghetto again. Tickets took the form of small betting slips that were carried back to policy collectors. In certain areas, the slips took three-by-five-inch dimensions and were yellow in color, with carbon paper in between each for transference. The players kept the originals; delivery staff retained the copies. Other runners, called "pencils," avoided the use of tickets altogether, preferring to write bets on their arms to carry them back to stations. If cops suspected them of the illegal courier work they conducted, with one lick of a fingertip and a smudging of the lead, the evidence was destroyed. A brilliant, select few were even more cautious: They memorized the numbers they took from dozens of customers to collectors in waiting. The collectors supervised daily management of the games. Employing the collectors as their management staff were the bankers, who financed the games.

More than a few names became legendary as both heroes and villains in numbers lore. Ellsworth "Bumpy" Johnson, for example, rose in status from bodyguard to esteemed king of Harlem when he stood his ground against a white organized-crime invasion led by thug Dutch Schultz, who attempted to move in on the numbers racket overseen by Johnson's boss, Stephanie St. Clair. At the height of the Martinique native's 1930s reign before she was jailed, St. Clair shoveled in as much as $50,000 a week. The vast appeal of the numbers that made the game so lucrative was the fact that its penny and nickel bets could be turned into hundreds. Lower-level managers generally took about 10 percent on winnings, while the bankers took about 25 percent. Apart from its employment of runners and managers throughout various urban centers, the racket was largely supported by the black community because of the reciprocal role its organizers played in building institutions. Philanthropic gestures by policy makers provided supplemental income to the businesses that fronted for numbers stations. Additionally, hospitals, social organizations, and other well-regarded establishments received assistance in keeping their doors open and making their services to the public available. Policy organizers were seen as men and women of the people.

The people themselves—as in the players of the game—were a study in techniques. A number of them paid regular visits to the neighborhood fortune-teller. They saw the investment in a card reading or similar "psychic" interpretation as worth the potential in gaining an edge against the thousands and thousands of other competitors. Many times they learned their own supposed lucky numbers but with the convenient disclaimer that was less certain to determine when their particular combination would come up on The Wheel or in the harness results. Also popular was the use of "dream books" as a policy betting method. Available at the local newsstand, the publications assigned specified numerals to words and images, which allowed the players to translate their thoughts and experiences, as well as what they could recollect from psychological activities during sleep, into bets. Among the male gamblers, it was not uncommon that digits the books represented with specific sex acts or erotic associations were favored, particularly when attractive women took their bets. A brown-skinned, wide-smiling sister with firm, round breasts might be appealing on more levels than one. Others simply guessed at the winning three numbers, while there were those who preferred to take a variety of other sources as their bettors cue. Suggestions from children. Significant dates denoting births, deaths, marriages and other events. License plates from wrecked vehicles. Hymn boards in churches. Not even the preacher's Sunday-morning sermon was too sacred for a player with a hunch or premonition about the real meaning behind chapter 3, verse 14 from the book of Proverbs in its reference to the virtues of wisdom: "For the merchandise of it is better than the merchandise of silver, and the gain thereof than fine gold."

Ever watchful in the black community, police officers were, nonetheless, subject to bribery. Now and then there might be a raid of a policy station for the sake of appearances, to show the mayor and taxpayers that they were earning their salaries. Then, in keeping with the well-orchestrated routine, as well as keeping their sources of pocket-liner available to make police work a bit more rewarding, law enforcers made sure the arrested parties bonded out. The law, however, wasn't the only element for which there was a need to be on the watch. Any number of street predators would lie in waiting for the chance to catch a runner slipping in his diligence, maybe stopping for a soda or taking a shortcut through a dimly lit area. A female runner without male protection would be considered an easy mark. Likewise, a manager spotted fucking up a security measure at a policy house could expect to face a pistol or maybe get a lump on the head. Particularly for a frustrated bettor, the temptation loomed to wade more deeply in the waters of the underground. Or for a predator to knock off any sucker wearing a target.

Court records would later tell the story of January 25, 1961, when Donnie hooked up with two acquaintances, Donald Hawkins and Marion Higgins. Hawkins and Higgins lived in the same neighborhood on East Canfield. The three men had set their sights on a numbers house not far away. Katherine Peek was minding the money when Donnie and his accomplices made their way into the place. Donnie was carrying the gun. The men made their intentions clear. As their robbery got underway, they heard the sounds of a child coming from another room. Fearing what might become of her as the victim of a crime, Peek quickly got an idea. She asked if the men would allow her to excuse herself, just so she could stop the baby from crying. Feeling momentarily vulnerable to his true humanity and probably confident that she was frightened by the sight of the weapon he held, Donnie gave her permission. In the brief moment that Peek disappeared from sight, she called the police. A month later, Donnie, Hawkins, and Higgins were in Recorder's Court. Donnie pled guilty of assault with attempt to rob while armed. He and Hawkins were sentenced to two to twenty years at the state prison in Jackson. With its imposing gun towers, Jackson was the largest walled prison in the country at the time. Higgins was given three to four years at the lockup for a lesser charge of felonious assault. Donnie would be released on parole in 1962.

But the relatively brief incarceration did little to affect his penchant for get-rich-quick schemes. Robbery simply wasn't his forte. In another episode, Donnie found himself stopped cold and looking every bit of a damned fool. The same type of short-sighted judgment led him to his only arrest by an authority worse than any policeman. Donnie liked to hit the racetrack now and then, and on this day he blew all his shit. He seemed to pick any horse but the winner. So, dejected and desperate to get a fix, he left. Then, packing two pistols, he decided on what should have been an easy mark for a stickup job. Myrtle made it her practice to attend weekly bingo. It was one of her pastimes and ways of getting out of the house. She was first shocked and then furious when, as she and others were assembled for their evening game, a young man busted into the hall demanding money. It was Donnie. As he gripped his weapons, he may not have realized his mistake until she was already upon him. Maybe he was too strung out to see her approaching.

"Boy, put that down! What the hell is wrong with you?"

Unfazed by the presence of the handguns, Myrtle slapped his face twice, as if he were still just a child. Donnie had fucked up, and it damn sure wouldn't be the last he heard about it from his mother. But at least her intervention might have saved him a trip to the County.

His failure notwithstanding, Donnie's quest for the big hustle, for untouchable criminal status, was as driven as it had ever been after he got home from Jackson. So it was by fate and circumstance—combined with their common interest in money—that Donnie became close friends with a woman who was called Miss Hattie. A senior citizen who was given the respect of an elder in the community, Miss Hattie was of an age that had brought her wisdom in more ways than one. The old lady operated an after-hours establishment and whore joint. She supplemented her income through the production and sale of bootleg corn liquor. Joanie would look down toward Miss Hattie's house and laugh at the sparrows in the alley when they tried to fly after pecking at fermented corn kernels that had been thrown out. Miss Hattie shared her bootlegging secrets with Donnie, who decided he would become a distiller and sell his product to other after-hours social clubs in the city, like Miss Hattie's. But having paid little attention to his science classes, he knew little about chemistry. The first makeshift still he opened for production overheated and exploded. Donnie would try again. Determination could be a motherfucker.

"*United States of America* versus *Donald J. Goines*."

The clerk at the Court of the United States for the Eastern District of Michigan announced the case in traditional fashion. Not "*United States of America* versus *Bad Ass Nigger*" or "*United States* versus *Public Enemy Number One*." Even without the flashy introduction, however, Donnie knew it: This was the federal system. For better or worse, he had finally made it to the big time. It was another sentencing day, August 2, 1965. The Honorable Wade H. McCree Jr. took to the bench and addressed the young man before him.

"Mr. Goines, you are before the court for the purpose of having sentence pronounced for the offense of unlawful possession of a still, sugar syrup solution, and unlawfully working in a distillery, of which you were found guilty by a jury when you were before the court previously."

From the beginning, it had looked pretty bad for Donnie. The prosecution spelled out its allegations against him: Under an assumed name, Donnie rented the lower section of a two-family flat in Detroit. His landlady declined to lease him the upstairs, but gave him the keys to it. Donnie later advised her that he had done the service of letting the upper for her to Johnnie Young, a brother who worked for Ford. Later investigation determined that no such person existed. A fed had placed the building—and presumably its occupants—under surveillance after he smelled fermenting whiskey coming from the home. Donnie was spotted at one point carrying two cement blocks into the second-floor apartment and was seen the following morning with his cousin, Curtis Stewart, entering the upstairs together. They remained inside for about twenty minutes. Not long after that, an agent watched Donnie and Curtis deliver fuel to the site of the distillery. While he was on his way to work later the same day, November 23, 1964, authorities for the government's Alcohol and Tobacco Tax Division took Donnie into custody. Curtis was snatched up just as quickly. Having acquired a search warrant, feds went into the flat and investigated. There on the second floor, a 110-gallon drum, or "stillpot," was discovered propped up on blocks of cement. Inside the stillpot were 100 gallons of sugar solution. Also strewn about the upstairs were "various barrels and jugs, some with whiskey mash inside," a report indicated. Empty sugar bags littered the apartment, and some were even found on the first floor, where Donnie was a tenant. There were all the makings of a fledgling criminal empire, and Donnie, the would-be king of it, had been at the center. The government felt there was "ample" evidence to convict him.

Donnie had waited as Curtis faced the judge. He didn't make out so bad, all things considered. Two years probation sounded like a sweet deal compared with federal jail time. The harshest words Curtis received had been issued for a matter completely unrelated to the whiskey still.

"Oh, you have got a bad traffic record," McCree told him. "In fact, it is a disgraceful record, I would say. There appear to be ten traffic violations over about a ten-year period."

"I don't have any moving violations," Curtis interjected.

"Pardon me?"

"I don't have any moving violations in there."

Curtis explained that the offenses were for illegal parking during the time when he worked as a cab driver. After that, McCree decided maybe the background data in front of him wasn't so bad. "There are some problems of nonsupport of your family, which troubles me," the judge briefly lectured. "There are no felony convictions, though. You have never apparently committed a crime involving moral turpitude or requiring felonious intent."

A few more moments of questioning revealed that Curtis was training at Washington Trade School to become a steel fitter. In five days, he would complete the program. Soon, he was practically shining like new money in the courtroom. Curtis was going to get a chance to avoid being locked up. Instead, he'd get to take his pick of two or three available job opportunities at a rate of almost three dollars an hour. He could virtually walk away as if the federal conviction had never even happened. McCree closed with the remaining words of the lecture he had begun a few minutes earlier: "Now this is in consideration of the following facts: First, you have this family to support; second, you are re-training and you are equipping yourself to do this in a better way; and third, you have no previous felony convictions. Now, this means that if you make good, as we hope you will, we will close your file two years from now. If you violate any of the terms of your probation—and the probation office will give you those terms, and they are my terms—you will be brought in and the sentence here will be executed. Is that understood?"

"Yes, sir."

Curtis received instructions to make his probation appointment, and was told to have a seat. Judge McCree took his time as he prepared to share and discuss what he had learned about the remaining defendant in the courtroom. Donnie listened. "I have ordered a presentence report, which was prepared for me, and it reflects a great deal about your background," McCree began. "I will tell you what it shows me. It is not altogether good. Oh, we start in 1958—there are some minor ones earlier—with a charge of Junction City, Kansas, where you received a twenty-day sentence, apparently involving some prostitutes working for you in and about an army base. Do you remember that?"

Donnie spoke up. He attempted to cast the charge in a not-so-seedy light.

"I did twenty days for vagrancy, your Honor."

"That was the official charge," McCree noted, "but it is reported as involving that kind of activity. Then, in Flint, a twenty-dollar fine and thirty days for frequenting a house of prostitution. Do you remember that?"

"Yes, sir."

"Then July 19, 1959, in Detroit, Michigan, a ten-dollar fine and thirty days in the house of correction on a charge of aiding and abetting. Was this the same kind of activity?"

"Similar."

Judge McCree continued studying the report as he spoke.

"I am overlooking some driver's license and other traffic offenses. Then we get a serious one. January 25, 1961, assault with intent to rob, armed, in the Recorder's Court, this is Judge Murphy—was that Judge George Murphy?"

"Yes, sir."

McCree seemed less than impressed with what Donnie presented of himself. It wasn't hard to foretell what was to come. Leniency didn't seem detectable in the judge's tone.

"A conviction and a sentence of two to twenty years in Michigan State Prison with parole June 25, 1962. It is reported that you carried a gun and that you and two other persons were involved in an attempt to rob a known numbers operator. I suppose if you were paroled in 1962 for two years, the parole had just expired when this offense took place."

Again, Donnie tried to mitigate the damage.

"Sir," he started, "maybe six months. I got off on early parole for good behavior."

"Six months." McCree pondered. "Yes, that is a bad record, Mr. Goines, for a young man thirty years old."

Actually, Donnie was still twenty-nine. His birthday wasn't for another four months. Finally, McCree laid the real numbers down for him.

"The maximum penalty for this offense is $1,000 or two years on count one; $10,000 or five years, or both, on count two; $5,000 or one year, or both, on count three; and $1,000 or one year, or both, on count four.

"Now, I will ask you, have you anything to say or any evidence to present in mitigation of punishment before the court pronounces sentence?"

Donnie gathered a response: "Well, I am working now is about all I can say on my behalf. You have my record. I would like to get the opportunity to get probation, if possible."

"I can't consider you for probation in light of this record. You have had prior felony convictions, and you know your way around. This isn't the first time. This was a pretty deliberate thing . . . It appears that you owned the apparatus. It was a pretty deliberate thing. This isn't a little activity."

With that, the judge served Donnie his fate. He was given eighteen months with "a chance to impress the parole authorities." The federal pen at Terre Haute, Indiana, would become his new home for a year. Such was the penalty for criminal ingenuity. Myrtle and Joanie made the trip from Detroit to visit their forever-felonious loved one. Donnie would appeal the sentence but with little success. Through his lawyer, he contended there was insufficient evidence and argued that McCree had erred in his reading of a statute to the jury. Too little, too late was the appellate court's response. It was 1968 when he returned to society again. Although he couldn't have known it, Donnie's incarceration might have been a blessing for his own protection this time around. For truly only God could have known what might have happened if Donnie had been walking the streets in the early hours of July 23, 1967.

There was a private club, located above the Economy Printing Co. on the east side of Detroit's Twelfth Street, which called itself the United Civic League of Community Action. The name might have meant damn near anything, considering the times. After all, the brothers, the sisters—even a lot of the white kids—were for action in the community. Cops said, however, that the only rhythm jumping off in this joint was booze. The club might have been one of the clients Donnie had in mind when he set up the whiskey still. The so-called blind-pig establishment was suspected of illegally serving drinks after 2:00 A.M. Officers prepared to raid the building in a mission to shut the motherfucker down. It was still about an hour before daybreak, and there was still a crowd inside the club. Completely unsuspecting, the partiers not only were minutes away from being arrested as the police took their positions but also were about to become a part of one of the most horrific incidents in the city's history. It was Sunday.

The cops made their move inside. As they began to bring out the 82 people arrested, a crowd of about 200 formed and started talking shit to the officers. When words began to seem insufficient, somebody threw a bottle. Then a brick that went crashing through the back window of a squad cruiser. Soon afterward, a fire was started and the first of what would be hundreds of stores was looted. Detroit was about to be turned upside down. The crowd at the scene had become a mob. Officers had few options for calling in backup because it was nearing the end of summer and a number of cops were on vacation. As a matter of fact, there were only a scant 193 policemen patrolling the entire city of a million-plus at the time when the chaos broke out. As it became obvious that the officers were overwhelmed, looting and hell-raising spread along Twelfth, down to Fourteenth, Linwood, Dexter, and Grand River avenues. One of the city's two black congressmen, John Conyers Jr., braved his way out into the madness. He was joined by Detroit's lone black councilman, Reverend Nick Hood. The pair hoped that they could use their rapport and influence with the people to get them to disperse. They hoped to preserve what was left of the community. But nobody was hearing it. Not today. By that evening, mayhem had spread to the East Side. Plundering and devastation was rippling through neighborhoods like tremors. Glass was shattered from countless numbers of windows and doorways. Debris covered the ground as if it were confetti dropped from the sky. Entire walls were removed, and roofs were torn off by fire devastation. Piles of broken wood, concrete, and ashes collected on the floors inside of what remained from blocks of ravaged structures.

Probably hundreds saw the uprising as an opportunity to feed themselves and their families by breaking into grocery establishments. All of the shelves in an A&P supermarket were ripped off. The canned goods and meat had all been stolen from the store. Barbecue sauce covered the floor like blood where a diligently arranged condiment display had been knocked over by raiders. Just about every Caucasian-owned-and-operated business in the community was a potential target, as the rebellion's participants—many genuinely frustrated, many just opportunistic—determined that this was a chance for them to take what had long been rightfully theirs. Liquor was hauled out of drug stores by the case, while others went after more valuable possessions. In the warmth of July, the victorious could be spotted strolling up Twelfth with fur coats draping their bodies. Then there were armfuls of clothing and jewelry, TV sets, radios, and other small appliances that traveled just as conspicuously. And thefts progressed to physical violence. Perhaps finding little worth the take at his shoe-repair shop, attackers seized the old man who owned it, pulling and dragging him out into the middle of the street, where he was beaten without mercy. A number of shop owners in the hottest areas chose to arm themselves, fearing that their livelihood was at risk. Black shop owners placed signs with sayings like SOUL BROTHER in their windows, reminiscent of the blood used to mark door frames in ancient Egypt during the Passover. They hoped, in some cases vainly, that the mobs would spare their businesses, just as it was told in the Old Testament how the Creator spared the lives of firstborn children in Hebrew homes. No one could truly know what could be expected. Unlike the '43 disturbance, this was an explosion of tensions and hostility that was borne of economic circumstances and was directing itself primarily at the city's economic foundation.

As early as Sunday afternoon, it had become clear to Mayor

Jerome Cavanagh that the hurricane of larceny, arson, and violence was too large for city resources to contain. Known for his liberal social views, the mayor had won 85 percent of the black vote in his 1962 election at age thirty-three. He had successfully solicited $230 million in federal funding, a good chunk of which was slated for programs that would benefit the Negro community. Only a year earlier, *Look* magazine had named Detroit an all-American city, under Cavanagh's leadership, so it came as rather a shock that his constituents were in such an uproar. The best of his mayoral efforts had clearly been insufficient for the legions of folks who scoured the neighborhoods in search of places to burn and pillage. The efforts had clearly been insufficient for the sense of security lost among shut-in families who feared that this rage might literally spill over into their backyards. Too afraid to go out and buy bread and milk. Unsure of whether they would even find bread and milk at the market, judging by the damage they saw broadcast on their televisions or heard discussed on their portable radios. Governor George Romney was notified by his legal advisor that Mayor Cavanagh had requested assistance. The situation escalated when sporadic sniper fire was reported. Danger had begun to rain down from rooftops. His police force rendered ineffective, Cavanagh sought the support of the National Guard. On Sunday evening, a curfew was issued between the hours of 9:00 P.M. and 5:00 A.M. Romney declared a state of emergency, sending 400 state police officers and 7,300 Guard members into the eye of the storm. Many of the reserves, however, were ill-prepared to respond to such a major uprising. These were young men who, in numerous cases, had only joined the Guard to avoid being drafted and sent to Asia to fight in the Vietnam War. They quickly proved no more capable of containing the violence.

By now it was Monday, and the mayhem had not ceased in twenty-four hours. At 3:00 A.M. Romney phoned the vice president, who referred him to Attorney General Ramsey Clark for assistance with federal troops. But it was Tuesday morning by the time 4,700 airborne soldiers actually arrived at the danger zone dressed in full battle gear. As Washington debated with Romney— and the head of the troops who'd traveled to the scene attempted to demand a written request for assistance for the second time—the number of blazes being set reached its peak. More than 600 fire alarms had been registered, but firefighters were forced away by the raiders before they could do any good. The wasted time may have also cost one man his life. Among the thousands of black folks who had taken over the streets, Walter Grzanka, forty-five and Caucasian, might have been risking his safety when he ventured into hostile mob territory. But it probably became apparent that he, like plenty of others, was only out to take advantage of the situation when he headed toward a market on Fourth Street. The decision would cost him. Grzanka became the first casualty of the massacre when he was shot by the market's owner as he ran away from the building. His take seemed a paltry one for having put so much at stake. Cops found nine pairs of shoelaces, four packages of tobacco, and had seen cigars in his pockets.

Now it was Wednesday morning. As in '43, armored vehicles, including tanks, rolled down public streets. All of the additional military enforcement was beginning to make an impact. More than 3,000 arrests were made that day. So many people were taken into custody that the county jail had no chance of holding them. They were transported and housed in Jackson, at Milan Penitentiary, in surrounding county facilities, on city buses, in the police garages and gymnasium, and even at the public bathhouse on Belle Isle. It was a haphazard system of holding suspects, but considering the circumstances, no method would be quite perfect. With such a critical matter on their hands, it would have been hard to fathom that officers David Senak, Ronald August, and Robert Paille could find the time to terrorize three young men who were not even involved with the chaos. Seventeen-year-old Carl Cooper, eighteen-year-old Fred Temple, and nineteen-year-old Aubrey Pollard were among several black men gathered at the Algiers Motel with two white women, who had records for prostitution. Cops responded to yet another report of sniper fire Wednesday night, this time at the inn. Cooper, Temple, and Pollard had records for only minor offenses, and there was no conclusive evidence that they committed any offenses or provoked police in any way, upon the officers' arrival at Algiers. Still, all three of their lives ended that night. They had been shot at close range with 12-gauge shotguns, two autopsy investigations concluded. August, Paille, and Senak were handed a menu of charges in connection with the murders. Cops were said to have used racial and sexual taunts as they knocked around motel guests, taking the property under siege. Though August and Paille admitted to shooting two of the young men, they claimed self-defense, and no one was ever convicted. The whole affair resembled a northern version of the Scottsboro episode but with a more immediate and tragic ending for three teenagers.

The final death toll in the uprising numbered forty-three people, nearly all civilians. Thirty-three Negroes had lost their lives, along with ten Caucasians: Thirty were killed by the police or military, three by private citizens. Two looters perished in a blaze, and a firefighter and civilian died when they came into contact with fallen power lines. Almost 500 people were injured, including police, firefighters, National Guard, state police, U.S. Army members, and civilians. More than 1,600 fires had been reported during the course of the uprising as a total of 14 square miles was gutted. And a startling 7,231 people had been arrested: 6,528 adults and 703 juveniles, of whom the youngest was ten years old and the most senior a white man of eighty-two. At least half of the accused had no criminal record. Only about 3 percent of them ever stood trial, half of whom were acquitted. Property-wise, the figures were also staggering, with about 2,500 stores looted, many demolished completely. Kresge, Red Robin, and Charles Furniture were among businesses that literally burned to the ground. Despite the various efforts of residents near the war zone, even homes were reduced to ruins. Close to 400 families were displaced. Figures ranging from $40 million to $80 million covered the estimated amount of loss. Emergency crews had brought assistance from across the river in Windsor, Canada, and from as far as ninety minutes away in Lansing and Flint. It had taken a force of about 15,000, including the federal troops, to squash the last of the violence. The city had literally wreaked havoc in a rebellion against virtually every established form of authority that existed, beginning with those first police officers who emerged from the blind pig. The All-American city had become the site of what was called one of the worst uprisings of the twentieth century.

Significant underlying factors were suggested as the major contributors in the eruption. After all, the after-hours bust was not, by any means, the first raid cops had conducted in the city. Detroit's police presence, however, like the presence of law enforcement in other urban locations, was seen as a manifestation of racism rather than equal protection for all citizens. Officers were paid to secure the black community, but who secured the community from them? Dating back to the '50s, units known as the Big Four patrolled neighborhoods in large, black squad cars. The units consisted of a uniformed officer—often a Negro, who was the driver—and three intimidating plainclothes men filling the passenger seat and the back. Officially, Big Four's function was to search the streets for major felons. In reality, they fucked with whoever they wanted to, and black men were not uncommon targets. One of the most enduring bastions of white privilege in the city was the police department. While there had been attempts to create change, in 1967 the force was only 5 percent black. So as the melee outside the blind pig morphed into a half week of destruction, the community began to look like occupied territory. An overwhelming majority of the officers, reserves, and federal troops were Caucasian, and their presence, in spite of the situation's urgency, was largely regarded as typical repression. Reports of police brutality had been frequent when nationally known activist H. Rap Brown appeared at a conference just weeks before the rebellion. Maybe nobody knew whether he was selling rhetoric or speaking what he felt in his soul, but his words proved prophetic. Though he was still affiliated with the Student Non-Violent Coordinating Committee at that time, Brown's speech had nothing to do with holding hands, marching, or singing "We Shall Overcome."

"Let white America know that the name of the game is tit-for-tat, an eye for an eye, a tooth for a tooth and a life for a life," he urged his listeners. Brown was actually paraphrasing the martyred revolutionary minister Malcolm X, who, a few years earlier, had

Donald Goines in his U.S. Air Force portrait; he enlisted as a
teenager by using a doctored birth certificate.
(Courtesy of Marie Richardson)

A tiny "Donnie" (front, wearing hat) enjoys a warm summer
day with family and friends circa 1940.
(Courtesy of Marie Richardson)

Donald Goines (right) as a teenager posing with
an unidentified acquaintance
(Courtesy of Marie Richardson)

"Big" Joe Goines was more affectionate toward his daughters,
Joan (right) and Marie (not pictured), than his son, Donald.

(Courtesy of Marie Richardson)

Donald Goines's older sister, Ceolia Marie, dressed
for Holy Communion circa 1944

(Courtesy of Marie Richardson)

December 15, 1938   October 21, 1974

In Loving Memory

of the late

DONALD JOSEPH GOINES

Monday, October 28, 1974
11 A.M.

CHURCH OF OUR LORD
JESUS CHRIST
2341 E. 7 Mile
Detroit, Michigan

Cover of funeral obituary bearing the author's
most published photograph; it incorrectly lists Goines's
year of birth as 1938 rather than 1936.

(Courtesy of Marie Richardson)

Despite his early self-consciousness, women found Goines attractive and charming as he matured into manhood; here, he chats with an unidentified young woman.
(Courtesy of Marie Richardson)

Donald Goines's parents, Joseph and Myrtle, in their Detroit home circa 1970
(Courtesy of Marie Richardson)

Demonstrating his rapport with the opposite sex, Donald Goines embraces a willing, but unidentified, photo subject circa 1968.

(Courtesy of Marie Richardson)

Another child, 2 adults killed

■ Why? Families seek answers following death of 6 Detroit youths in 6 days.

By Scott Bowles and Ann Sweeney
THE DETROIT NEWS

A 3-year-old Detroit boy and two adults were shot to death Saturday when their car was sprayed with bullets in a normally quiet west side neighborhood.

Donald Goines III became the sixth Detroit child slain in six days when someone opened fire about 3:30 a.m. on the 9200 block of Grandville, police said. Also killed were Donald's godmother, Tanya Smith, 24, and an unidentified 26-year-old man. Smith's boyfriend, Earl Sheppard, 26, and an unidentified 24-year-old woman, were wounded.

Witnesses and relatives said the boy and four adults were in a car in the driveway of a home owned by Smith and Sheppard when someone opened fire. The car lurched forward, breaking through the driveway gate and coming to rest in the back yard.

Donald Goines "already knew he wanted to play basketball."

Donald's grandmother, Thelma Powell, drove by the house Saturday morning, hoping to make sense of the killing, the third multiple slaying involving children in Detroit in a week.

She left more puzzled than pacified.

"Why are the children the ones to

Please see Victim, 4A

The death of Donald Goines III, the apparent unintended victim of a drive-by shooting attack, saddened Detroiters. Like his grandfather's murder, it remained unsolved in 2004.

(Courtesy of *The Detroit News*)

included "a head for a head" for emphasis in the original statement. Neither choice could be mistaken in its meaning. "Motown, if you don't come around," Brown continued, "we are going to burn you down." Similar rebellions had preceded Detroit's in Harlem and the Watts section of Los Angeles, both only a few years in advance. One person died in Harlem, while L.A. lost thirty-four. Both episodes, like Detroit's, had been sparked by the actions of police. It was clear that young black folks, in particular, held cops in contempt. Combined with a 30 percent rate of joblessness for the brothers and sisters who were eighteen to twenty-four years old and the intensifying poverty of certain neighborhoods, what appeared to be selective law enforcement had made for combustible chemistry. Yet in the aftermath of the uprising, one public survey indicated that Caucasians saw the black community as entirely responsible for having "worse jobs, education and housing than white people." Firearm sales increased from the previous year's rate by 90 percent, as fear, rather than reflection, permeated Caucasian neighborhoods. Rumors of random violence committed by black assailants ran rampant by the end of the year. The city witnessed the beginnings of white flight to the suburbs.

Romney later expressed his feelings about the causes and conditions that precipitated the morning of July 23, 1967. He didn't blame it on unruly niggers who had created their own lack of opportunities so they could have an excuse to raise hell and terrify good, decent, God-fearing white folk. Romney was more thoughtful with his analysis. He reflected on the construction of expressways and urban renewal, which had translated into urban removal for poor residents who had been "bulldozed out of their homes." Of course, they had no prospects of fleeing to the suburbs because of residential restrictions that were still being illegally enforced, in spite of the Orsel McGhee housing discrimination ruling almost twenty years prior. Many of the displaced, noted Romney, had been pushed out into the Twelfth Street area, which became too densely populated, "so when that incident occurred, it was a spark that ignited the whole area." Others suggested that the raid itself had been unnecessary. Officers might have conducted a less aggressive operation to accomplish their goal, particularly since they were making a conspicuous bust in an area that already boiled with stress and simmered with discontent. The person who lobbed that first brick resented the show of force and the manner in which it was executed. And he or she was obviously not alone in the sentiment.

Donnie had developed no particular affinity for the law or its enforcement, but he had not reached the point of acting out violently toward the cops. So while he might not have been involved with the physical confrontations and violent resistance that took place during that week, had he not been incarcerated, Donnie would have recognized other opportunities to make some personal gain. Addicts stole goods to trade in for smack, as heroin use experienced a surge in the late '60s. The rebellion was a free-for-all to those who thought they'd shoplift as much as they could carry out of a store. Of course, there were the few unlucky ones who chose establishments supervised by men with firearms. But fate had arranged things so that Donnie would have to sit this one out. He began serving his time and adjusting to his new surroundings. Whether at Jackson, Terre Haute, or elsewhere in the country, prisons were, more or less, operated in similar ways. Still, the inside of a correctional facility could feel like a whole different world. Particularly for a junkie in need of his dope fix.

The Joint

Most of the prisoners who came out of the wards seemed happy to be going. They grinned at each other, joked with men in other wards. All of them had something in common: they were either smiling or laughing loudly. A passerby who didn't know would have thought the men were going home. He would never guess that they were all on their way to the state prison. But that was the way the county jail affected a man. After staying there any length of time, the men were glad to go to prison, just to get away from the sorry food, the sorry sleeping conditions, the unwholesome closeness of a lot of men shoved inside a small ward with nothing to occupy their minds.
—White Man's Justice, Black Man's Grief, Donald Goines

I Heard It Through the Grapevine" hit No. 2 on the *Billboard* record charts. It had originally been recorded by the soulful Marvin Gaye but was first released by Gladys Knight & The Pips. "Standing in the Shadows of Love" by the Four Tops peaked at No. 6. Gaye's rhythmic duet with Kim Weston, "It Takes Two," reached No. 14. By the time Donnie made it to Terre Haute, acts from Motown Records had ruled the world of rhythm and blues for nearly a decade. Little Stevie Wonder, The Jackson 5, the Miracles, The Temptations, the Four Tops and a roster of others were rapidly becoming superstars, by virtue of their association with the Motown Sound. While Donnie had been out hustling with women and schemes, a young music lover and entrepreneur named Berry Gordy was hustling songs. Detroit-born Gordy had briefly worked for Ford, but he recognized his more creative talents as a writer and gained some notoriety penning such tunes as Jackie Wilson's 1958 hit "Lonely Teardrops." Wilson, another Detroiter, developed such smoothness and composed stage presence that Elvis Presley once asked him how he managed to give an energetic show and still avoid sweating during his performances. Associations with budding legends like Wilson would eventually become old hat for the young entertainment visionary. After borrowing $800 from family members, Gordy converted a two-story house on West Grand Boulevard into what became Motown's original recording studios.

Borrowing its name from the city's reputation as the motor capitol of the world, the fledgling label was a fresh and new concept for the recording industry. Groups and solo artists were manufactured in assembly-line–like fashion, from talent recruitment to grooming, style, and etiquette training, which went hand-in-hand with the final studio sessions and presentation of its acts to the public. And the public was a receptive one. The Motown vision involved scouting out talent from local neighborhoods and helping to transform the unseasoned, often church-trained performers into professional entertainers. Many of these would-be icons were just out of high school and had not received the benefit of instruction in singing or choreography, let alone how to give interviews to the media. They were taught the kinds of crisp, synchronized movements and choreographic flair that became a signature for Motown headliners. With work and patience, they began to exude the confidence of the celebrities they often became. In promoting the grandeur of its expectations, Motown flashed a sign in front of the headquarters: HITSVILLE USA. During the company's thirteen-year Detroit era, before it relocated to California, it created the image of the city as an urban epicenter, from which romance and glamour could emerge. Befitting its company moniker, the record label singularly made music one of the industries most closely associated with its hometown, second only to automobile production. The label became a significant part of the local economy, employing not only singers and musicians, but songwriters, publicists, account representatives, and various additional behind-the-scenes staff members. It was a company that achieved success unlike what few in Detroit could ever hope to gain.

The Motown Sound was a distinct one. Instrumentally, it combined strong bass lines and a grinding back beat with various forms of gospel-influenced call-and-response vocals and thoughtful, poetic lyrics. Subjects mainly touched on romance and youth but eventually expanded to include politics and societal conditions. The songs were largely collaborations of songwriters, producers, and musicians. What resulted were tunes, both exciting and mellow, slow and upbeat, that were played on car radios, at high school dances, and in popular nightclubs all over the globe. Motown tunes often told stories without much narration. Listeners could relate to just about every situation or experience discussed in the music. Socially, Motown was even becoming a revolutionary force: At the height of its popularity, it would have been difficult to find many white households with teenaged residents who didn't hum the label's tunes, sing lyrics they knew by heart, or dance in front of mirrors, imitating the classy steps they saw performed. After all, the messages were quite universal and delivered in the sweetest, most pleasant-sounding ways. There was rarely a Motown recording—at least one that got much attention—that sounded angry or brooding. Far more rhythm than blues, which were always more personal and culturally specific in a place like the United States, songs made Motown performers idols across the color line. A perfect example was "Dancing in the Streets" by Martha & the Vandellas. Punctuated with celebratory tambourines, blaring horns, strings, and piano, the tune had a triumphant tone about it. The lyrics spoke nothing of the turbulent remaining days of the civil rights struggle or the ongoing challenges that were evident in the lives of most who fit the social demographic of Motown group members. Instead, they spoke of a carefree response to the tense mood of the nation. Uninhibited, aggressive physical expression through dance.

As the end of the '60s neared, however, the tone of the music became less saccharine. Artists proved they had not forgotten where they came from when they touched on themes close to the experiences of the neighborhood kids they had been not too long ago. Releases like the Supremes' "Love Child," recorded from the perspective of a poverty-stricken, bastard girl, and "I'm Livin' in

Shame," also by the Supremes, were a radical departure from their earlier No. 1 hits, like "Come See About Me." The music began to reflect the thoughts and concerns of a generation. It was practically unavoidable that Donnie would become a fan of Motown. He made it a point to get into whatever was hip and happening, because being a square would never do. Though he would have just as soon seen a pretty Detroit girl like Diana Ross, whom he had noticed in the neighborhood, turned out on the street, he appreciated the musical talents that performers like Ross shared with an adoring public. A lot of the brothers who were locked up had been nurtured on the sounds of Motown. But in the joint, of course, they were prevented from enjoying most of the luxuries that had been available on the outside.

The United States Prison at Terre Haute was built in 1940. Located not far from the facility was Indiana State University, established nearly a century earlier in 1865. Terre Haute was founded as Fort Harrison in 1811 and grew as a river town, thanks to the currents of the Wabash. Situated in a farming and coal-mining region, the city's population hovered around 70,000 at the time when Donnie was committed; however, he and the other inmates living at the 1,000-or-so-capacity federal facility were not regarded as part of the community. In fact, Donnie was more obscurely, yet formally, known as No. 24871. By now, he was no stranger to the jails. His record accurately fit the term *habitual criminal* before the phrase became common in discussions of the correctional system. He virtually lived with a foot in the joint for several years. At one point, Marie had written him from Oklahoma, where she lived with her new husband. She expressed support for her brother and urged him to use the time he was sentenced to better himself.

"Hi Donnie," she wrote. "Well, Mama received your letter and we were so glad to hear from you. I do hope the adjustment wasn't too difficult. Donnie, if you are allowed to attend school, please take advantage of it. I'm sure it will be a tremendous help to you. Just do as you're told and I'm sure you'll come out alright." She promised to visit Donnie when she returned to Detroit, which she told him would be soon. While at Terre Haute, Donnie took steps that seemed to fit his sister's suggestion. He enrolled in at least one course that dealt with health and medical sciences. Judging by his 100 percent score on a true-or-false and multiple-choice quiz, it might have been difficult to believe he was a high-school dropout. He correctly answered such technically worded questions as "Is an internist an expert in diagnosis?," "Is an occultist a nerve specialist?," and "If a friend of yours seemed inexplicably depressed and unhappy, would you suggest a visit to a psychiatrist?" He also correctly identified the roles of an obstetrician, cardiologist, orthopedist, and pediatrician. Donnie's performance was an indication of his capacity to learn more legitimate means of surviving than those he'd come to rely on in times of freedom. He must have been proud of himself because he kept the test for several years.

The joint had become a place of self-education for many of the brothers who found themselves incarcerated. In fact, prison was often seen as the virtual equivalent of college for young men who had rejected the dictates of society, particularly the educational and social standards that evolved from European, Christian value systems. While it was true that they had been charged and convicted of crimes, it was an undeniable reality that race and class thought patterns were still a major influence on the workings of American criminal justice. Many a convict was led to the conclusion that his incarceration was a direct result of the intolerance of a government that had never really intended for him to have freedom to begin with. Prison was not so terribly different from a slave plantation, after all. Corrections officers served as the equivalent of overseers. Inmates were dressed as they were told to, fed only when it was determined that they should eat, and disciplined in various ways when they disobeyed. A number of deputies even took their racism to work with them and acted out their aggressions toward black prisoners in much the same way slave owners sought to maintain control.

Such an analysis, of course, was partially flawed. Those who were lawfully convicted had forfeited their rights because they had violated state code and statute. Their freedoms had not been arbitrarily restricted based upon their race. Yet the similarities and the recognition of the suffering a hateful environment had put them through were enough for many a black man to reach the common conclusion: He must learn what he was not taught about himself and other cultures in order find pride despite hostile circumstances. As a result, inmates frequently turned to African history, Islam, the study of Eastern philosophy, and other sources of enlightenment that had never been offered to them in school.

One of the enlightened, Huey P. Newton, had been accused of murder just a month after Donnie's arrival in Indiana. Newton, who cofounded the Black Panther Party barely a year earlier, was charged with killing an Oakland police officer and wounding another in a shoot-out. The Panthers were inspired by and became students of Third World nationalist struggles, such as that of Fidel Castro in Cuba and Mao Zedong in China. Based in California, the Panthers sought to link the black liberation movement with other freedom movements throughout the world. They patrolled neighborhoods with shotguns as a show of unity and as an indication of the protection they were willing to give citizens who had been victimized by the very law enforcement assigned to serve them. They made publicly known their intention toward "defending our black community from racist police oppression and brutality."

Imprisonment, however, became an effective weapon in the government's battle against so-called subversives, who had nerve enough to assert their rights to humanity by methods that did not include pleading on bended knee. Apart from any preactivism encounters with the law, such as Newton's unrelated prison terms, Bobby Seale, Eldridge Cleaver, Fred Hampton, Assata Shakur, and numerous other revolutionaries spent time in the joint. A major casualty of the jail-as-a-weapon strategy against Panthers and other freedom fighters was Elmer "Geronimo" Pratt, a Vietnam War veteran, who brought his courage and experience to the movement. Pratt would spend nearly three decades incarcerated after he was convicted of murdering a white couple on a Santa Monica tennis court, in spite of the fact that he was 400 miles away at the time. This could be proven by the government itself, which had placed Geronimo under surveillance. The bureau's notorious Counterintelligence Program—COINTELPRO, as it became known—was designed to neutralize the efforts of organizations and movements that threatened the status quo. Through the use of internal disruption, character assassination, false propaganda, outright violence, and the criminalization of actions in pursuit of change, the FBI achieved measurable success. By imprisoning the most fiery and charismatic young leaders, it was possible not only to disturb the momentum of energy created by their words and behavior but also to discourage their supporters with the threat of lost freedom.

As a number of their own fearless and sacrificial soldiers experienced life behind bars, the Panthers took notice of the devastation that imprisonment was creating in the black community at large. The American judicial system was inherently biased in its treatment of people of color, they concluded. All things considered, how could any true justice be administered on stolen land? In each and every courtroom where defendants had ever been sentenced to prison or death, there was a red, white, and blue flag: a reminder of the very crime. A reminder that the country had been captured from dark men and women, colonized, and redistributed in the fashion that Europeans—who disregarded and changed all the pre-existing standards of order—saw fit for establishing law. The system was literally poisonous at its root. Its primary beneficiaries, even hundreds of years later in the 1960s, were the progeny of statesmen, judges, and the most common of Caucasian ancestors, whose skin and citizenship came with entitlements. It seemed no wonder, then, that as men and women of color continued to press for equal treatment toward the end of the modern civil rights era, they consistently found themselves charged with landing on the wrong side of the law. Among the nation's general population of incarcerated criminals, there were frequently the common denominators of race and class status. In and of themselves, such circumstances should not have mattered when applied to those who had actually broken the law. Still, the quality of legal representation, efficiency of trial proceedings, and even the actual determination of sentences were all consistently related to the physical complexions and economic standing of those who were charged with crimes and brought to court. Those immediately receiving any advantage from the output of the flawed process were a part of something scholars and writers began to call the prison industrial complex.

In this setup, the industry, much like automobiles or fast food, was driven by its manufacture. The product was the prisoner. And the industry of confinement was one that involved dollars and the potential for financial gain. When a prison was built, there was the promise of contracts, and with contracts often came the promise of renewals. Not including the requirement for staff to supervise the inmates, the possibility of stable employment in various capacities came along with operating a correctional facility. The inmates, in turn, could be selectively used—some would have argued that they were deliberately exploited—to provide cheap labor that ultimately would profit the state. In a particular way, the operation was just as seamless as Henry Ford's assembly line, for while it wasn't due to the same demand for access to capital, no one anticipated there would ever be a problem with filling prisons. Crime was a reliable source of lawful capitalism. The Panthers recognized such social patterns, and within a few years they released their party's ten-point program. No. 9 stated:

> *We want freedom for all black and oppressed people now held in U.S. federal, state, county, city and military prisons and jails. We want trials by a jury of peers for all persons charged with so-called crimes under the laws of this country* [italics used for emphasis]. We believe that the many Black and poor, oppressed people now held in United States prisons and jails have not received fair and impartial trials under a racist and fascist judicial system, and should be freed from incarceration. We believe in the ultimate elimination of all wretched, inhuman penal institutions, because the masses of men and women imprisoned inside the United States or by the United States military are the victims of oppressive conditions, which are the real cause of their imprisonment. We believe that when persons are brought to trial they must be guaranteed, by the United States, juries of their peers, attorneys of their choice and freedom from imprisonment while awaiting trial.

Conversely, imprisonment and the death penalty were about the extent of the government's deliberation as it pertained to addressing upheaval and disorder. There was no room for socialist analysis, particularly among the capitalists who thrived off of the industry and all its imperfections. In accordance with their approach, at least one of the system's internal failings was actually a plus of sorts where helping the prison machine to function was concerned. Recidivism, as the process of repeat offense and reentry to the world of corrections was called, accounted for a sizable portion of the inmates. First-time criminals could see the inside of the penitentiary, of course, depending on the nature of their legal violations; however, recidivistic felons found themselves in a routine. Existing outside of the law became a means of survival, as time spent in the joint, without significant preparation for handling freedom, only made assimilation more difficult. Interaction with more seasoned criminals behind bars could also be partly blamed for the return rates: Just like university courses for undergraduates, the pursuit of worldly education was valued by students of the street. Donnie's recidivism was significant in the manner of its progression: He had climbed, or perhaps descended, from incarceration in state-run facilities to serving time in the federal pen. The distinction was not necessarily a reflection of the seriousness of his crimes, at least probably not by what the woman he'd held a gun on at the numbers house would have said. It was more of a subtle statement about the tolerance levels that robbery and alcohol violations were assigned by lawmakers. It screamed irony. One act was pretty much stamped as unsurprising, typical nigger misbehavior, while the other could be compared with literally taking money from the government. Having the balls to try to beat Uncle Sam at his own damn hustle. And the government's hustles were not ever supposed to be fucked with.

Another small percentage of the inmate population was actually comprised of ex-government personnel. Vietnam War veterans, having returned home from yet another American confrontation in Asia, found it hard to get their lives back on track in many cases. For vets of color, the odds of unemployment and poverty were even greater than for the average. Out of desperation and, in a number of instances, feeling completely abandoned by the society and institutions they had supposedly fought to help preserve, some chose crime as a last resort. After standing on the front line in Southeast Asia, as one of the popular Motown artists put it, they found themselves at the back of the line when it came to getting ahead. Hundreds of thousands of U.S. troops had arrived in Vietnam by the mid-1960s. As the decade moved along, the term *alienation* could be frequently heard in discussions about the political and social climate of the country. The so-called ideological and more liberal "left" was generally given the responsibility for this phenomenon, which came to be associated with ongoing race problems and protests against the war. Those who wore the "hippie" label, students of higher education, and any scattered number of genuinely progressive thinkers were coming to reject the image of America they had grown up learning about. Believing in. Pledging allegiance to. It seemed a bullshit notion that in a freedom-loving society, young men were being drafted into military service to kill and be killed, if necessary, for the nebulous purpose of gaining victory in foreign lands. World domination was the farthest thing from their minds. And there was little defensible logic to believing a government that appeared so preoccupied with it could stand for anything resembling civility and democracy. Divided opinions about action in Vietnam affected American communities more dramatically than had any war before it.

More outspoken leadership elements had been critical of any black involvement in the conflict as far back as 1963. It was outrageous, according to their position, for more men of color to die in defense of a nation that had consistently refused to protect their women and children from the dangers they lived with on a daily basis. One *New York Times* reporter would note that, among those who refused to outright condemn the war, there was still hesitation when it came down to encouraging black participation in the effort. For the first time in America's history, his article noted, "national Negro figures are not urging black youths to take up arms" in the hopes that they could "improve the lot of the black man in the United States." Apparently, after decades and generations, truth had sunk in. Black soldiers could go wherever they were commanded, bleed rivers on enemy soil, lose precious limbs, leave their loved ones widowed or fatherless, and it would never make a goddamned bit of difference in the level of respect or acceptance in first-class citizenship afforded their people. In an abstract confirmation of this reality, even the predominantly white local draft boards wasted little time in doing what they could to preserve discrimination. Board members preferred to conscript young black men. In 1967, 64 percent of those eligible were drafted, compared to only 31 percent of eligible whites. A year later, black recruits made up about 10 percent of the total United States military but only 2 percent of all officers, typically suggesting the establishment's belief that they were best suited to receive orders rather than issue them. For reasons more appropriate than one, the black servicemen referred to one another as "blood." They formed the battalions that engaged in violent jungle warfare with Vietcong.

Just as Donnie had experienced years earlier, the Asian terrain also produced recreational dangers. Hash, marijuana, and smack were again made available to the soldiers, both black and white. Just as Donnie had, a good number developed addictions and ultimately experienced life-altering consequences. When they returned to the States, they counted themselves among the junkie populations that struggled between the listlessness of drowsy, drug-induced nods, to survive in the ghetto. At home, black popular opinion turned steadily in opposition to the war. The objections continued, even as Washington ordered growing numbers of men to join the fray of troops already engaged. Meanwhile, the questioning of authority at home gradually rippled from the civilian population all the way across the ocean to the ranks of the servicemen. With the eastern-accented words of Vietnamese disc jockey Hanoi Hannah working to sweetly persuade them that they shouldn't be there—even as she entertained them by playing all their Motown favorites—the black soldiers began doubting the wisdom of their superiors. Along with the Mexican recruits, they faced the most perilous and thankless combat assignments. Where they had once been excluded from battle, now they were virtually condemned to it. Black soldiers wound up as about 20 percent of the American battlefield casualties. The last units wouldn't leave Vietnam until 1973, two years before the conflict's end. As the American occupation increased, though, so did enemy resistance.

Back in Detroit, the younger brothers who came up behind Donnie found themselves eligible for draft duty. As it was elsewhere in the country, men between their late teen years and their mid-twenties were assigned numbers based on their birth dates. The higher the numbers, the less likely they were to see a uniform. Those unlucky enough to get lower numbers could reasonably expect to get their "greetings," formal mail-delivered notice from the government that they were being drafted into the military. The notice contained details about where and when they should report for their physical and psychological evaluations. Those who were called "conscientious objectors" had generally already written the draft board: several pages detailing their reasons, religious, personal, or otherwise, for opposing the war and explaining why they should be exempt from service. Those who reported for induction and refused to take their oath to join, sometimes even after a little coaxing from a sergeant, were allowed to go home. But it was usually just a matter of months before they were visited by FBI agents, flashing badges and asking, "Are you . . .?" Following the normal arrest procedure and booking through county jail, they were scheduled for trial on the charge of violating the Selective Service Act. The end result found objectors locked up right along with the general prison population, including those convicts who had fought their way out of the jungle and made their way back alive. There had been a couple of other options besides the one that led to the joint. Full-time college students could legally avoid the draft. As could anyone willing to leave the country. A number of Detroiters simply chose to cross the river to Canada. And then there were the young men who opted to enlist in the reserves, figuring it was unlikely that they'd ever have to see battle. Of course, if they had been among the Michigan National Guard sent to Detroit in '67, they learned different. Among the brothers who went to the joint, however, refusing the call was viewed as a badge of honor. All that derogatory talk about draft dodging was meant to sting when it came from the mouths of politicians, but it didn't mean shit in the community or in prison, the one place that might have been, in many respects, just as tough as a tour of duty.

Less-celebrated resisters didn't make out as well as boxer Muhammad Ali, who was convicted of draft evasion before the Supreme Court reversed the judgment. Many ate, slept, and shared toilets with dope dealers and robbers until they were released for their crime of consciousness. As convicts of various backgrounds and persuasions came and went, Donnie got through his time. It was hardly a secret that drugs flowed into the prison population, but it was difficult to tell what, if anything, Donnie may have been able to score under the watchful eye of federal guards. Yet, when he left Terre Haute in September 1968, it appeared that he was shooting up the same amount of heroin he had used before he had been sent away. His drug of choice was now common contraband on the streets. The more things had changed in some corners of the world, the more they had managed to stay the same. That same year when Donnie came home, the *New York Times* published a quote from Orville Hubbard, the notoriously racist mayor of Dearborn, a Detroit suburb. "I favor segregation," he told the newspaper, "because if you have integration, first you have kids going to school together, then next thing you know, they're grab-assing around, then they're getting married and having half-breed kids. Then you wind up with a mongrel race. And from what I know of history, that's the end of civilization." Hubbard's comments left at least a vague impression of political maturity since his less-reasoned statement in the 1950s: "If whites don't want to live with niggers, they sure as hell don't have to. Dammit, this is a free country. This is America." Regardless, this was one politician who would never admit to bigotry, instead explaining himself with declarations like "I just hate those black bastards."

Seeming to waste little time, Donnie used the American freedom, of which Hubbard spoke, to get himself right back into legal
trouble.

By 1969, he had been sentenced to do time closer to home, at
Jackson once again. Cops arrested Donnie for attempted larceny.
No sense in lying, he figured. As he had the last time he was sent
out to Jackson, Donnie pled guilty. The record from this particular
bid of just over a year gave a cursory look at who he had become by
age thirty-three. The "birthdate" box still carried that false recording of 1934, which he'd listed in order to make it into the air force.
Under "religion," the abbreviation "Cath" had been typed right
next to "education," accompanied by the number of his last grade,
nine. Interestingly, Donnie's occupation was listed as truck driver,
though he'd not worked for any serious length of time at anything
besides hustling. His "intelligence," presumably according to standard measurement, was named at an even 100. "Marks & Scars"
was a section used to help identify an inmate if ever there was any
confusion within the population or possibly in the event of an escape. Donnie's track marks on both arms were prominent from
years of shooting smack. He had picked up a couple of tattoos
along the way, too. They served as distinguishing features but had
a significance that was limited mostly to his knowledge. There was
the snake on his left forearm. Joanie and Marie could remember
how nasty it turned with infection when he first came back from
getting the design. It had taken a while to heal. On his upper right
arm was a woman's name, Edna. Nobody his folks seemed to recognize. Not the mother of any of his children. Lord knew that
among the ladies with whom Donnie became acquainted, he had
plenty of names to choose from. Nevertheless, Edna earned
a place in his heart. She simply wouldn't remain a part of his life.
Otherwise, the data didn't reveal much for him to be proud of.
Apart from its mention of his military experience, the record left
doubt as to whether Donnie had ever served anyone or anything
besides himself. But things were about to change.

Donnie began exploring talents and potential that he had neglected for maybe as long as it had been since he attended school as

a child. First, he toyed around with artwork. Then, at one point, he got into essay writing; prison was an obvious place where the men inside had lots of time to reflect and consider their opinions about the world beyond. One of Donnie's proudest moments was when a piece he had written about the civil-rights work of Martin Luther King was printed in the prison paper. During one visiting day, Myrtle gave Donnie a typewriter she had hauled out to Jackson as a gift she thought to be a practical one. Through it all, he was still her boy. In the meantime, Donnie had gotten turned on to a particular author. The writer had traveled a path that Donnie could well relate to. They shared a connection to the city of Chicago, though they'd lived there at different times and had vastly different experiences. The writer grabbed Donnie's attention. Robert Beck became known as Iceberg Slim during his time in the underground. Older than Donnie, he had made a career of pimping and had also spent time in the joint. It was about 1969, the year that Beck's first autobiographical writings were printed, when Donnie developed an interest in his stories. Beck brought a raw reality about the codes of hustling and street survival to the reading public. This reality was largely unknown to brothers and sisters who had not witnessed and participated in the illegitimacies that folks like Donnie had. To the uninitiated, a pimp was often just a punk nigger who didn't want to get a real job and behave like a real man. A stable was a group of dirty, loose women who didn't have the good sense to keep in their own pocketbooks the money they earned while lying on their backs. For plenty of men in the joint, however, these were the people whose lives they had grown up trying to emulate. In fact, the particular series of events that had led a number of them to prison might have even had something to do with an episode that began as a simple business matter between a pimp and his woman. Donnie, for example, probably never considered the federal violations he was committing when he took his ladies to work out of state. A piece of ass was a piece of ass, whether in Michigan or Alaska. Others who'd gotten into the habit of handling women might find themselves dealing with less directly related charges pertaining to money, violence, or even corruption

of children, who might lie about their ages to get away from malev-
olent homes.

Iceberg Slim's writing brought a lot of this into focus. His following was primarily in the circles of those who could relate or of those
folks, black or white, who wanted to keep up with popular culture.
Beck's books carried simple and self-explanatory titles like *Pimp*
and *Trick Baby*. Both eloquent and worldly, by the time Donnie
would leave the joint for his final time, Beck would be widely recognized as a celebrity. He was invited to lecture about his past life,
present observations, and thoughts on current events at college
campuses, and he was interviewed in such prestigious publications
as the *Washington Post*. He became a fascinating figure, whose
very presence was intriguing. He earned the respect of many who
were open-minded enough to try to understand the perspective of
a different kind of man who maintained a measure of credibility in
the types of neighborhoods that produced him. An interview Beck
would give to the *Los Angeles Free Press* offered a glimpse of what
those who paid him any serious attention might find fascinating.
Beck told the reporter of a question-and-answer session: "The best
pimps that I have known, that is the career pimps, the ones who
could do twenty, maybe thirty years as a pimp, were utterly ruth-
less and brutal, without compassion. They certainly had a basic hatred for women. My theory is, and I can't prove it, if we are to use
the criteria of utter ruthlessness as a guide, that all of them hated
their mothers. Perhaps more accurately, I would say that they've
never known love and affection, maternal love and affection. I've
known several dozen, in fact, that were dumped into the trash bins
when they were what? Only four or five days old."

While he was quick to say that he loved his own mother, he acknowledged that he must have resented her on some level because
of the neglect he had demonstrated toward her through the years
that led up to her death. He further elaborated on the events and
disappointments that ultimately led him to retire from the dubious
profession: ". . . I remember when I was a young pimp—and that's
where the thrill is—when one is young enough and . . . ill enough
to want to be a pimp. That's where all the glory is, when one is

playing Jehovah, so to speak, and learning his craft. Then, oddly enough and disappointingly enough, when one learns to control eight or nine or ten women, then all the luster, all the glory is gone. It's much like learning to ski. One just does it automatically. Then, of course, all the clothes and diamonds and the cocaine and the girls, it isn't really important. There is a vacuum that is filled by the joy of learning the intricacies of being a pimp. But it was the greatest letdown because I was reaching always."

Donnie grew to respect Iceberg Slim's words. He had become familiar with the conquests and defeats that came along with living in the underground. It was a realm in which only a few people were genuinely suited to thrive. Where—as Beck pointed out—the thrill and exhilaration were all in the pursuit. Where betrayal in the midst of camaraderie was nothing unusual. Where death could be the price of one mistake. It was, in all reality, a lonely place in the end, even for the most successful and prosperous hustler. What Beck was doing, though, was a new kind of hustle. He'd been in the life, made it out of the joint. Now he was simply telling about it. Seemed like a good, legal way to get paid. And Donnie had plenty of stories in him, authentic tales of moral corruption and judicial repercussions. He decided to try his own writer's touch. From inside the walls of Jackson, though it was far from the most creative of surroundings, he began putting words on paper. Employing Beck's style, he wrote in the first person, filling both sides of hundreds of sheets of lined, loose-leaf paper with variations on details he had lived and witnessed:

One of the older pimps staying at the hotel I moved into pulled one of my girls. In spite, I shot at, and [copped] a 24-year-old white girl from his stable. This proved to be my undoing. Not really having any connections for a white girl, I allowed her to lay around my pad for about a week, before having Boots take her down to one of my whorehouses on Hastings. The nigger tricks went crazy over her. It lasted exactly five days before the police caved the door in, taking my whores to jail. I knew that my cathouse was busted before the police came out the door with the girls . . . The judge gave me a 7½ to

15-year sentence. I looked at that white bastard in a state of shock. I had come to court looking to get probation, but instead [I was] sentenced to prison. I hadn't known the white girl two weeks!

My lawyer had promised me probation because of my age. How could a seventeen-year-old kid [possibly] corrupt a 24-year-old woman? If anything, he had told me jokingly, while standing in the hallway before walking into the courtroom, the judge would give her [ninety] days for teaching a young boy my age bad habits.

With no experience as a published author and no professional guidance, however, getting his work into the right hands was a shot in the dark. He thought maybe the newspaper would be a good place to begin in finding the feedback he sought. Donnie thought he'd send a sample to the *Michigan Gazette* back at home. Staff member Mildred Pruett responded. She addressed the letter, including Donnie's inmate number, 104882:

Dear Sir,

I am very sorry to be so late in writing to you. First of all, I would like to let you know that I did receive your material and found it to be very, very interesting. The second [thing] that you should know is that I am no longer with the *Michigan Gazette*. In fact, there will no longer be a *Gazette* published here in Michigan. Do not let this upset you because within a few weeks, or even less, I will be editor of a much better paper and a much larger paper. The paper will come out once a month, and by it being a larger paper, there will be room for much, much more of the type of things that you are writing about. You can look to hear from me in about two weeks from now. I will give you the new office address and all the information that you will need. I will say again that I am sorry about being so long [in] writing, but I am sure that you know how it is when there are legal ends to be tied.

Donnie might have taken offense to the "legal ends" reference, but it was probably just a poor choice of words on Pruett's part.

She seemed genuinely receptive to the possibility of publishing his contributions and genuinely impressed by her efforts. But whatever the level of her interest had been, the journalist was apparently able to provide little beyond her cordial letter. Donnie wouldn't be released for another year, and it wouldn't be his last attempt at starting a new, legitimate profession. As the end of his term drew near, he grew more resourceful in his research. Eventually, he got the idea to look up the company that published his new inspiration, Iceberg Slim. If they could put Beck's name out there, surely they could do the same for Donnie. And poking around among the familiar resources back in Detroit produced few results. A prophet was said not to be without honor except in his own country; a prophet in prison couldn't realistically expect to do much better. Donnie put another one of his queries together and mailed it off from Jackson. Then he waited. After going to the joint more than once, the ability to pass time became routine. Without any question, freedom was still desired and missed, but in its absence, a sort of numbness inevitably set in. And inmates who had already done a bid or two for any length of time tended to learn to use that numbness to their advantage. Days would begin to resemble one another, often to the point that they seemed not to matter. The less a man kept track of days, the more quickly they seemed to accumulate. It could get tougher to maintain mental conditioning, though, when the end of a term was in sight.

Donnie was discharged from the Michigan Department of Corrections on December 1, 1970. Just two weeks before his thirty-fourth birthday. He left the penitentiary, this time never to return. Heroin use on the streets and in the neighborhoods of his hometown had increased while Donnie was locked up. The city now operated four clinics where dope fiends could go to be treated with methadone, a smack substitute. Yet, after regaining easy access to sources who could help him score the drug, Donnie would not sign himself in at any of them. Like Marvin Gaye and Tammi Terrell sang on the radio, wasn't "nothing like the real thing."

Publisher

One chapter for me to remember is the one dealing with young people nodding . . . Again, try and reveal the sickening, the madness, the horror of drug addiction in the ghettoes . . . It's a fact that whitey has no idea of just how many young, black men are getting dependent on heroin.
—Typewritten memo, titled "Black Rage of Hatred," by Donald Goines

Holloway House Publishing Company was located in a rather inconspicuous, gray building at 8060 Melrose Avenue in Los Angeles, not far from the rocky hills where some of the most extravagant homes in California were tucked away. A person would have to really know the city or be involved in the book business to make an association upon hearing no more than the business's name. Holloway House went about its work rather quietly in the commercial district that served as its neighborhood. Not even too many of the taxi drivers who cruised the area could identify the building from recollection in the way they could identify nearby bars, restaurants, or shopping outlets. Actually, there was no real reason for employees to attract attention with their comings and goings. It was a relatively small operation, especially in light of how the best-known publishing companies ran their business in the 1970s. Most of them were set up a full coast away in New York City. They drew upon the history of the area as a diverse and creative community, along with its status as a destination for artists, musicians, and literary types. California, on the other hand, was more driven by the entertainment industry as a professional component. Hollywood beckoned countless numbers of aspiring actors, screenwriters, directors, and models. Film and television had become increasingly lucrative business with the likes of Warner Bros., Universal Studios, MGM and 20th Century Fox maintaining a significant presence in the region. Dozens of features were produced annually and distributed to movie theaters nationwide, while everything from Bugs Bunny cartoons to Coca-Cola commercials and episodes of *Columbo* were regularly broadcast into America's living rooms. Of particular interest was the new genre of movies and TV shows generated in Hollywood that reflected a different stage of black attitude and thought emerging in the real world. Shiftless, shameless, and embarrassing characters were replaced with proud and defiant heroes and antiheroes. Even the complexions of those who made it to the screen became darker as actors like Sidney Poitier broke into the mainstream. A Bahamas native, Poitier learned his way around the stage, originating the role of proud but stubborn Walter Lee Younger in the Broadway production of *A Raisin in the Sun*, Lorraine Hansberry's acclaimed play. Later, he costarred opposite white actors and actresses in the films *In the Heat of the Night*, *To Sir with Love*, and *Guess Who's Coming to Dinner*.

Poitier represented a sort of quiet, reserved, and dignified black man. When his police officer character in *In the Heat of the Night* was asked by racist southern cops how he was addressed among more liberal colleagues, he kept his cool, but replied: "They call me Mr. Tibbs!" In contrast, another darker-skinned crime-fighting character MGM brought to the screen preferred lines like "Don't let your mouth get your ass in trouble." Director Gordon Parks's second feature-length film, *Shaft*, actually netted enough profits to help deliver MGM from financial ruin. John Shaft, the movie's title character, was a take-no-shit private detective. Operating against the backdrop of rough Harlem streets, Shaft took on an assignment to search for the kidnapped daughter of a gangster who wanted her safely returned to him, no matter the cost. Ultimately, Shaft enlisted the support of an old friend and a militant group to rescue the girl from mobsters. His character was well-received by young, Afro- and dashiki-wearing audiences, many of whom had no real concept of what it was like to see themselves as anything besides black and proud. The detective embodied a sense of confidence that had come to characterize the generation. Richard Roundtree, the handsome actor who portrayed Shaft, brought forth the image of a brother who was very different from what had previously been projected onto the screen. With a composed and laid-back approach to his work, an ability to move comfortably across social boundaries, and a fearless manner of handling his enemies, he represented the first black action hero. Shaft was a consummate professional. His style of speech and dress and his relevance to the times found a connection with the urban public. Boys throughout the country wanted to wear leather jackets and refer to one another as "baby" in place of their actual names. Adding appeal to the film was a soundtrack that featured the contribution of soul composer Isaac Hayes. When his baritone vocals roared in, inquiring "Who's the man that won't cop out when there's danger all about?" those in the theater were all too happy to give the song's response: "Shaft!" The movie also garnered positive critical reviews, despite a few others that dismissed it as tacky and sexually clichéd. The Motion Picture Guide praised Parks for his concentration on Shaft's "humanistic elements," which brought "depth to the super-slick detective, showing other sides to his personality."

With so much cinematic excitement in the town, it was understandable that a little book company might not be the top competitor for the public's attention. Holloway House was more inclined to press others toward the forefront. Nothing was more valuable to aspiring storytellers than an outlet that would be dedicated in getting their words out to a readership. Equipped with the resources the company had available and a sense of what would draw attention to bookshelves, the folks at 8060 Melrose had the primary objective of cranking out paperbacks. The company did its own editorial production, distribution, and promotion of materials. If book enthusiasts had never heard of Holloway House, they worked to make certain that names like Louis Lomax, Robert H. deCoy, and

Iceberg Slim—as if it weren't already distinct enough—were familiar. Loads and loads of books by black authors had been purchased in towns where segregation was still law. In fact, Holloway House made a point of marketing its products in urban communities and unconventional places that might be better suited to unconventional stories. Paperbacks were made available at airports, on newsstands, and in liquor stores. Would-be customers who went looking for Holloway House titles at big, commercial bookstores would often be out of luck. Beck alone would sell millions. His first work, *Pimp: The Story of My Life,* became a legend in print, which highlighted the reflections and ruminations of the career Beck had embarked upon at the tender age of eighteen. The young woman handler had briefly attended Alabama's Tuskegee Institute at the same time that Ralph Ellison, who would become a more widely respected author with his book *Invisible Man,* had been a scholarship student there. Iceberg Slim was self-taught as a writer, and he combined whatever legitimate skills he acquired with the compelling personal observations and encounters that he documented on paper. With Holloway's publication of *Pimp,* he went as far as including a glossary of terms to assist those who would have been regarded as "square" in following the hip and quick language of his text. "Breaking luck" was a phrase defined as the first "trick," or client, that a whore received during her work day. A "mitt man" was "a hustler who uses religion and prophecy to con his victims," usually women. "Yeasting" was defined as a form of exaggeration. And "circus love": "to run the gamut of the sexual perversions." Then there were more universal terms: "horns," for example, were ears.

Though his publisher worked to give the book support, there was resistance. The *New York Times* didn't even have to consider *Pimp*'s content. When Holloway House tried to place an ad, the paper declined to accept it because of the title. Removing the one word that the *Times* advertising department found objectionable, however, would have changed the entire tone of the pronouncement. It was a sign of the times that Holloway House was giving something different from what much of the general public was accustomed to getting from a book producer. Revealing the story of a pimp's life turned out to be more than a notion. Yet, the company rose to the occasion. They continued a publicity effort to get *Pimp* a little play. Iceberg was booked as a guest on a popular L.A. talk show hosted by Joe Pyne. This was the move that created the buzz Holloway House had been listening out for. Phones began to ring at 8060 Melrose. The television appearance had generated a good amount of response. Enough, at least, to stir interest in the publisher's starring player. Suddenly, every bookstore in the city was contacting Holloway House.

As word-of-mouth spread, interest in the Beck chronicle followed suit. Holloway House was on the map, at least in a small way. In literary circles, on the other hand, any acknowledgment earned for the company by virtue of *Pimp's* success might have been regarded as tentative at best. There were relatively few critical reviews given to paperback releases by the book and features editors at major newspapers and media outlets. Stories were printed in the *Washington Post* and the *Detroit Free Press,* but they focused on the fact that Beck's work discussed a culture entirely unfamiliar to the American mainstream rather than on the merits of his word usage or his story content. The fascination, such as it was, essentially resulted from the very nerve that a legitimate company—and white-controlled, no less—would be bold enough to front this sort of storytelling. It was compelling stuff, but of the variety that members of the general public, outside the black community, might force themselves to be just as comfortable ignoring. It was the kind of tale that, at least subconsciously, they longed to not only read but understand. The black man. The stranger. The alien. The feared one. What the fuck could he actually have to say that was so completely unsanctioned by the established standards that dictated how he could and couldn't publicly express himself? And what if it actually had relevance? A thinking, articulate black man, particularly one with the capacity to commit criminal acts, could be a goddamned dangerous thing. If hundreds of years of conditioning hadn't been enough to breed into him a self-activated censorship switch, he could quickly become troublesome. He could be freely critical of the society that had helped produce him. The society that had nurtured his ancestors with fine food and free room and board on spacious, bountiful plantation land.

Beck's writing was largely symbolic of this back talk. *Pimp* was a form of literary insubordination. Not only that, but it directly challenged notions, stereotypical and otherwise, about the American image of black men and sexuality. The preferred racist belief was that they were helplessly sexual creatures who would fuck a hole in the ground in the absence of better options. They were controlled by animal instincts and loins that blazed with overwhelming, violent passion. Iceberg Slim was the big, black buck with a book contract. *Pimp: The Story of My Powerful, Menacing, and, Mostly, Large Dick* might as well have been his publication's title as far as sheltered Caucasians were concerned. The trouble with that image was that Beck had total poise and composure. He was in no way ruled by a lack of self-control. His ability to take command, as a matter of record, was a major asset. He worked with his brain more so than his body. After all, no pimp who got too caught up in the sexuality of a woman could successfully manipulate her. Beck had the qualities of a leader: charm, charisma, and determination. Furthermore, there could be no proper way to label a man with an IQ not far from 200 as a savage nigger. When he was an inmate, Beck could have probably been running the prison. Not only was he naturally bright, his presence was imposing. At six feet two, he had finesse, dressed immaculately, and beamed confidence. The author might have become Iceberg Slim, attorney-at-law, or maybe Alderman Ice in his native Chicago, had he chosen a political career. Crime had become, for Beck, a form of rebellion against the order set by that very class of people who would one day fear what he had to say. Indeed, the historical parallels would have likely been lost on his critics, but America was built by men like Iceberg, who essentially violated laws and reconstructed society according to their own needs and standards. Payback was a bitch. Especially when nobody saw it coming.

Probably without knowing, Holloway House managed to toy with a psychosexual dynamic as well. Through Beck's work, and the promotion thereof, a long-time taboo trembled in anticipation of breaking. Iceberg Slim was not shy in discussing his exploits with white women. How they became enchanted with him. Adored him. Eventually followed his orders and did his bidding just like any other bitch in his stable. It could be more than unsettling. It could bring about rage. But if Beck's publisher had been aware that it handled such combustible goods, there were no signs of discomfort. Holloway House was dealing in the type of merchandise of which other book companies wanted no part. While the white commercial publishers on the East Coast released perhaps one work of black fiction in a given year, Holloway was cranking out various writings by authors of color. They had books that examined the legacy of social activism and works that would have been regarded as less sensational, but Iceberg's tomes were the ones that cultivated a devoted following. Holloway House had found a niche and attracted a readership that attached itself to the company's literature. Still, not everyone approved. Even as he professed a genuine love and admiration for black freedom fighters, like Huey Newton and the Panthers, there were observers and cultural critics who felt Beck was doing the race a disservice. Primping and looking pretty on television while discussing in fancy language how he had snorted coke or turned out however many women was no form of behavior that could be seen as a source of pride, they argued. Panther member Eldridge Cleaver, whose award-winning book of prison essays, *Soul on Ice*, was published a year before *Pimp*, wrote on the topic of what Beck was arguably becoming, "The Negro Celebrity":

> By crushing black leaders, while inflating the images of Uncle Toms and celebrities from the apolitical world of sport and play, the mass media were able to channel and control the aspirations and goals of the black masses. The effect was to take the "problem" out of a political and economic and philosophical context and place it on the misty level of "goodwill," "charitable and harmonious race relations" and "good sportsmanlike conduct." This technique of "Negro control" has been so effective that the best-known Negroes in America have always been—and still are—the entertainers and athletes (this is true also of white America).

No one would have seriously argued that Beck was a legitimate contender for the "Negro control" seat white folks created for the select few establishment-approved individuals they might find occasionally useful. For one thing, the man known as Iceberg Slim had never been a member of the establishment. These were the figures who generally received the most attention from newspapers and television. Who were occasionally recruited by elected officials to deliver messages of solace or to beg for restraint, particularly during that turbulent '60s season of civil unrest. It was not necessarily an indication of their political bent but more a sign of their perceived appeal. Although Beck's notoriety paled in comparison to theirs, in some corners he was perceived as sort of a pretender to the throne, vying for attention from the very population he had rejected by way of his previous lifestyle. To these detractors, his books and public appearances were the equivalent of cooning—grinning and shuffling like an early-century minstrel performer. His impact on the culture, they felt, was to affirm racial stereotypes and legitimize them, which he undoubtedly did in the minds of at least a few dedicated racists, his intelligence notwithstanding. Critics among his brethren saw Iceberg Slim as an embarrassment, despite his impressive vocabulary and prideful semblance. Beck was capable of expounding on social theories, probably more effectively than most college professors. His testimony was more literally eye-opening than spiritually awakening, more raw than textbook or clinical, as when he wrote passages like: "My five whores were chattering like drunk magpies. I smelled the stink that only a street whore has after a long, busy night. The inside of my nose was raw. It happens when you're a pig for snorting cocaine."

In one sense, his critics might have reasoned, it was Beck who was now being pimped. Put out on the street to make money for a white-owned publishing company. His tricks were the folks who paid cash for his thinking-man's pornography and underground exposés. Those who attended his lectures were like the eager, horny customers found creeping in and out of the West Side Chicago apartment where his whores had worked lower-level units. The difference in this metaphor was that the adulation and fascination expressed by Iceberg Slim fans translated into profits for his big daddy: the company at 8060 Melrose. The evolution of Holloway House into what it would eventually declare itself, "World's Largest Publisher of Black Experience Paperback Books," began about ten years before Beck's literary debut. Ad men Ralph Weinstock and Bentley Morriss had become business collaborators by the late 1950s. They made their entrée into publishing with a couple of skin mags, which weren't so revealing at all compared with the girlie glossies that would line the racks of party stores in later days. *Adam* and *Knight* featured photos of teasing ladies, but *Adam* snuck in a bit of short fiction here and there to keep the pages engaging. Morriss, who hailed from Chicago, like Beck, had journeyed out to Los Angeles and done work for Warner Bros. studios. Weinstock was a Detroit native. Once he and Morriss decided they'd go the book route, they set up offices on Holloway Drive, right off of Sunset Strip, in 1960.

Against the entertainment-driven backdrop of pricey studios, spotlights, and celebrities, it made sense to put together a series of publications that would appeal to the community. Holloway would reflect Hollywood through the material it promoted. The lives of the nation's most fascinating personalities would be explored in print. As a result, the initial books published under the Holloway House imprint had little or nothing to do with black culture, street-influenced, consciousness-lifting, or otherwise. One of the first publications Morriss and Weinstock put out was *The Trial of Adolph Eichmann*. Others included biographies of the American literary icon Ernest Hemingway and screen contemporaries Jayne Mansfield and Daryl Zanuck. Holloway relocated to the Melrose address, a few stories of unremarkable, '50s-style brick architecture that slightly resembled a bus or train station at its entrance, in 1965. Morriss purchased the building, along with a warehouse not far from there, in preparation for the success he and his partner envisioned. At the time, they had never really even considered how the black experience might figure into that equation. Success for a publisher, quite simply, meant selling books, and the collective story of Negroes in America was still largely limited to one-sided, outdated encyclopedia entries and school textbooks. Apart from the literary voices of authors such as Richard Wright, Ralph Ellison, Margaret Walker, and James Baldwin, there was not much boldness or militancy to be spoken of in contemporary black writing. When Weinstock and Morriss witnessed the development of writers' workshops in Watts and at the University of California at Los Angeles, however, it was a whole new ball game. Holloway House recognized the opportunity to bring a raw and untapped element of creative expression to book buyers. An artistic revolution that reflected the attitudes of black men and women who were more influenced by Malcolm X and the Panthers than by the NAACP was underway. In the words of their poetry, essays, and manuscripts, a fiery energy could be read. It was an energy that could hardly be fueled by commercial exposure, which was the equivalent of selling out to the masses as far as those who generated it were concerned. Yet, with some effort, Holloway House was able to attract a roster of serious black writers, who desired, maybe more than anything else, to see their words in published form.

The submissions arrived at 8060 by the load. They put out journalist Lou Lomax's *To Kill a Black Man* in 1968. As what was apparently intended to be a serious critical work of nonfiction, it put forth an analysis of the lives and work of Malcolm X and Martin Luther King Jr., who was assassinated that same year. It did well sales-wise, but the book actually hurt its publisher's credibility. Lomax had been in the thick of civil rights movement coverage, becoming well acquainted with both of *To Kill a Black Man*'s subjects. He conducted interviews, wrote news articles, and got to be a familiar face in circles of men and women who dedicated themselves to making racial progress. It was Lomax who had previously written *When the Word Is Given,* one of the early books about the Nation of Islam, the religious organization that brought Malcolm X to prominence. But oddly, Lomax shed no light on his personal understanding or impressions of the Nation's one-time spokesman for his 1968 Holloway House release. In fact, he made no mention of the relationship. He had become an ally to the cause of the organization, which promoted black separation from Caucasian government, churches, and everyday life, in favor of building a new, independent society. Lomax had advised Malcolm X on how to put together the first oracle of the Nation of Islam, a newspaper called *Mr. Muhammad Speaks*. He had also made public appearances with Malcolm, debating with him the merits of the Nation's program. Lomax served, willingly, as a foil to help the organization present its ideas, which stood in stark contrast to what the mainstream civil rights groups generally supported. Despite this, *To Kill a Black Man* overlooked what those familiar with his role might have regarded as valuable insights.

What was worse for the company, though, was that the book landed Holloway House in court. A writer and editor by the name of George Breitman had first assembled the book *Malcolm X Speaks* in 1965, the year that the political activist and organizer was gunned down as he prepared to deliver a talk in the Audubon Ballroom of Washington Heights, near Harlem. Breitman's collection of "selected speeches and statements" included what became regarded as two of Malcolm X's most powerful and relevant addresses: "Message to the Grass Roots" and "The Ballot or the Bullet." Both orations mentioned the need for a greater level of courage and commitment to the struggle for racial advancement, rejecting the most commonly promoted beliefs about how people of color could rise in America as outdated or simply unfounded. Panthers had studied and quoted from *Malcolm X Speaks* like Sunday-school students reading the Bible. Breitman charged that Lomax had simply ripped off his editing for a good deal of *To Kill a Black Man's* content. He was furious, claiming that the reporter had done little original work for the book. The complaint was brought to court. Holloway House handled the matter and pressed forward, but to those in the black community who knew, the damage was lasting.

When Robert Beck showed up at the offices, he was like a ray of black sunshine. He was the personification of hip, but he carried himself in a way that commanded respect. No agent or representative spoke on his behalf. Beck was fully capable of representing himself; he was as comfortable in the boardroom as he had been discussing philosophy with Big Al on the front steps of the building where his ladies turned their tricks. Nothing about him suggested he had spent more time incarcerated than studying at Tuskegee. The unsuspecting white guys at 8060 had never encountered anyone like him. "This man could be a senator," Bentley Morris thought. He would become quite fond of the retired street player, eventually referring to him as "Bob." Like high-school cheerleaders spotting the football team captain in the cafeteria, Holloway's female support staffers would rush to the reception area to listen to Beck talk during his later visits. The editorial employees were impressed. After perusing ten to twelve pages of Beck's writing sample, they agreed that his work was of interest. Times in black America were changing, and the sentiments about leadership and social status reflected a heightened self-awareness. It wasn't seen as such a terrible thing for a brother to find his way through this fucked up world Caucasians had created in the best way he knew how. Holloway House believed there was an audience that could be tapped for response. Iceberg Slim was chosen to lead the company into a new genre of realism that wouldn't catch on with other publishers for years to come.

Having become a follower of Beck's stories while he was in prison, Donnie remained a fan after his release. As with other inmates, books in general had become more of a companion to him during confinement. More than they had ever been in Catholic or public school. When he left Jackson, Donnie decided he would put it all on the line and bare his creative soul. He informed the family that he had done more than reading while he was locked up. To prove it, he had in his possession a contract from Holloway House, dated October 19, 1970, almost two months before he had been released. The agreement was for the publication of *Whoreson*, the novel Donnie assembled while he was an inmate.

"You? A writer?" Joanie mocked in that incredulous tone that only a younger sister could achieve. Upon witnessing the hefty stack of handwritten manuscript pages Donnie had scribbled out in his cell, she looked at him as if he'd lost his mind. If Donnie had put the typewriter his mother gave him to use at all, it wasn't with this project. Now he was requesting Joanie's professional services as a transcriber.

"Whatever!" she said. Joanie was still getting used to the notion that her outlaw brother was seriously contemplating anything as straight and ambitious as a writing career. "But you are going to have to pay me big time!" Donnie informed her with assurance that she was going to help him become a famous author. It was a dream he felt prepared to pursue with every bit as much devotion and passion as he had employed while seeking infamy in the shadows of the law.

Joanie negotiated ten cents per page as her "big-time" rate of pay to put Donnie's manuscripts together. Her work was cut out for her. Her brother's spelling and sentence structure were quite the horror. Still, Donnie remained hopeful. Each day after coming home from her nursing job, Joanie would take her place at the typewriter. By now she was splitting her duties between employment and her sons, Michael and Patrick. Truly befitting a seed of Joe Goines, she had been working since she turned seventeen, but motherhood assumed a priority position in her routine. She would remain a single parent until she married David Coney, a man she met during a visit out of town not much later. It might have bothered Joanie to admit it, but she and Donnie were more alike in some ways than she chose to recognize. They both did things a little differently than what was most commonly accepted as the norm. In private moments when she was younger, Donnie had confessed that he was still sensitive about his complexion. Joanie was merely a couple of shades darker, a buttery tan rather than Donnie's pallid vanilla, but he wished he could be her color, he told her. Joan had listened, but what could she do? Besides wonder what other types of thoughts circulated through her brother's mind. Now, as they connected through his writing, she gained a certain sense. Her brother was troubled, but not hopeless. As long as he wanted better for himself, there was at least that small reason to be encouraged.

While the Holloway House editorial staff was still mulling over revisions and suggestions that they felt would get *Whoreson* in shape for publication, Joanie helped Donnie prepare *Dopefiend.* Its title described much of Donnie's life story of the previous twenty years. In his pusher character, Porky, Donnie revealed just how deeply he resented his heroin addiction. He occasionally referred to it as "wong." It sounded like a word he picked up overseas, but nobody seemed to know why he associated it with the drug. Wong was a fairly common Chinese surname, though, of course, Donnie hadn't been to China. In any event, he resented the fact that wong had beaten his ass for such a long time. So it was no coincidence that he made its emissary as repulsive as possible. Porky was not only blubbery and disgusting, but he evolved into a completely amoral demon amid ghetto trappings. As Donnie depicted scenes inside the pusher's apartment, he effortlessly drew from a body of knowledge. He had witnessed what transpired inside a dope house and had the ability to make it appear as a hellish, filthy place where pools of blood sucked out of junkies collected like puddles on the floor:

> *Jean pulled the needle out slowly. A look of rapture filled her face. She looked up and noticed Porky holding himself and watching her. Her eyes filled with scorn. She opened her legs wide and scratched herself. "Why don't you come over here, Porky, and let me rub some of this pussy up against your fat, black face." She spoke in a slow, tantalizing voice, all the while rubbing the sides of her cunt. The sight was beyond vulgarity. It was grotesque, even sickening, because as she sat there with her legs wide, a stream of blood mixed with pus ran slowly down her thigh.*

The graphic descriptions he gave his characters would make them unforgettable if they ever found an audience. Donnie and Joanie had become quite the team in their labor to get the package together. It was the first time either of them even thought about devoting such time and energy to this sort of task. The first time in Lord knew how long that Donnie had really begun to dream again, at least in terms of envisioning himself with any lasting prosperity. Ideas about robbery were a path that led him to prison. Making the whiskey that he wanted to sell for profit did the same. Pimping had been stressful work and ultimately contributed to the criminal record that influenced Judge McCree to send him back to prison. But in writing about the things he saw, heard, and did, there would be no laws broken. And the appeal didn't stop there. There was no clock to punch and no hard labor involved. Besides, it was a good gig for an ex-con to take, without the routine of sitting on the hopeful side of desk after desk in job interviews. Only about 65 percent of black men in the city were employed at the time; odds couldn't have been in a career criminal's favor. Everything was pretty much a hustle anyway, legal or otherwise, including the jobs of a lot of legislators who looked disdainfully on Donnie's kind. Writing would be a job that involved more benefits than drawbacks. Donnie packaged up his second manuscript and sent it off in the mail, hoping for the best.

As he awaited a response, for some reason, Donnie became discouraged. His two manuscripts were held in limbo for weeks. Maybe things wouldn't be nearly as easy as he thought. He went on a binge that lasted several days. The heroin that had both pacified and tormented him became more than a way to take the edge off. Donnie shot up like a man who had lost all hope. The track marks on his arms would never feel as neglected as his last remaining hopes. Then, finally, Donnie came out of his depression and regained focus. He sent *Dopefiend* off to numerous other major publishers. Nobody else seemed interested in the story Donnie had to tell. His sort of material was still widely regarded as without merit. He came up with the alternative plan of approaching a vanity press, which he knew would accommodate him as long as he paid their required fee. As discouraged as he felt, it had become important for Donnie to see his name in print. Then, as he prepared to make the move, he got word from 8060 Melrose. Bentley Morriss wrote to Donnie: He was interested in the manuscript.

Holloway House had put out a lot of black-interest books by this time, but these weren't the majority of their products. The company had become less celebrity oriented, publishing titles on subjects that ranged from gambling to popular history. Yet, with the help of works like *Dopefiend,* they would move in a more linear direction. About 90 percent of Holloway House's products would be black literature, stories that would sustain the company for many years to come. Donnie's manuscript intrigued the editors. They were struck by the vividness of his descriptions and the raw nature of the plot. Inside one of his manuscript packages, Donnie had placed a letter requesting the opportunity to meet his literary hero, if it could be arranged. His query was part professional and part fan mail. For whatever cause, the meeting with Beck he had sought would not take place, but Donnie could handle that. He was genuinely thrilled for the first time in what might have felt like an eternity. He was preparing to begin a brand-new career and, God willing, a prosperous one. Morriss set things in motion for the company to begin working with its newest recruit.

There was no way that Donnie's jubilation could be contained. He began formal collaboration with the staff on the *Dopefiend* manuscript, as they suggested character development, elaboration and expansion on his text. In a tone suggesting the same cordiality offered to more seasoned authors, an editor wrote Donnie in a letter dated December 29, 1970: "I hope your Christmas season was a very happy one for you. I've just reread *Dopefiend,* having gotten it back with comments from our publishers; I am even more impressed by the book. It's a heavy piece of writing. As with *Whoreson,* we would like to suggest a few minor revisions that we believe would improve the novel." They recommended that he add things like clarity, location, and "concrete details" to the story. In March 1971, he received a copy of his second professional writer's contract. The documents listed his residence at 17186 Maine, which was the address of a small, brick two-story, the most recent home Joe and Myrtle occupied. The agreement called for Donnie to deliver to Holloway House a revised, "completed" manuscript of between 50,000 and 75,000 words, a total that was likely more than he had ever written. It would be due in just shy of two weeks. For turning the job around, Donnie would receive a $750 advance. *Dopefiend* was scheduled for publication December 27. He would be paid in increments of $250, the first check upon his signing of the agreement.

Donnie might as well have been sitting on top of a cloud. There was no question now about the fact that it was all really happening. It wasn't a whole lot of money, but for each book sold, he would receive percentages. Then there were television rights, motion picture rights, syndication rights. Even a chance to see his writing translated into the languages of other countries. It was more than he could have imagined when he first decided to bring his characters to life on paper. The way he signed his name to the contract could be taken as an indication of the pride he felt in his accomplishment. Above the line marked "Author," near the spot where Bentley Morriss had made his identity known as Holloway House Publishing Co.'s representative, appeared the letters that spelled "*Mr.* Donald Goines."

West Coast

Goines seems to be looking at the poverty, urban decay and ruined lives, not as an amused god looking down on his creation, but rather as a street-level witness to the powerful effects of racism and poverty.

—Robert Skinner, author and librarian

Donnie's retirement from the streets came at just the right time. Hustlers of various types were about to catch hell with the advent of a new anticrime program. As Mayor Roman Gribbs settled into office, he was faced with—and forced to address—the reality of white flight from Detroit to outlying areas. Obviously familiar with the suffering that accompanied bigotry when it was directed at ethnic minority groups, the Polish Catholic politician had changed his surname from Grzyb when he was just a young man. He began his path to city leadership in law enforcement. Gribbs became a Wayne County sheriff and then an assistant county prosecutor. As his mayoral tenure began, just three years after the 1967 eruption, the city was in the midst of an exodus by businesses and home-owners that was creating an economic drain on the community. Cop that he was, Gribbs strategized according to the needs of pre-sumably upstanding, if anxious, citizens who remained in Detroit neighborhoods, in spite of their uneasiness. The mayor launched an all-out assault against criminals, including a controversial and dangerous undercover program called STRESS (Stop the Robberies,

Enjoy Safe Streets). Overseen by Chief of Police John Nichols, like the Big Four patrols that preceded it, the operation had a lopsided impact on city residents, not necessarily on criminals. Officers dressed in civilian clothes and made themselves conspicuous targets in high-crime areas. Their goal was to draw out the offenders and make arrests that would help reduce the level of fear in the community. But, for persons of color, STRESS proved to be stressful like a motherfucker. Arrests might involve officers violently subduing purse snatchers or petty thieves, which earned them a reputation as overly aggressive. The unit was creating more problems than it eliminated. Outraged civil rights leaders received numerous complaints from citizens who'd been roughed up or intimidated by STRESS officers. The radical black defense lawyer Ken Cockrel became a vocal opponent of the program. Perhaps one of the few things the lanky, broad-grinning firebrand loved more than taking on prosecutors was taking on cops. After STRESS officers killed several black youths, a public rally was held on September 23, 1971, to call for suspension of the unit. The squad hadn't even been established for a year. Yet, downtown Kennedy Square was filled with demonstrators who demanded an answer: If STRESS was put there to protect them, who would protect them from STRESS? Later on, more reports of shootings and related impropriety came to public knowledge. Then word got out that black youths actually died while in the custody of officers from the unit. STRESS, in one sector of the community, had become a source of *distress*.

The already strained relationship between the people and the police was being stretched to its capacity. Just as it had been in '67, the force remained predominantly Caucasian. And just as it had been in '67, those who felt most vulnerable to their authority were the men and women of color. Apparently disinclined toward worrying about the latter group, Gribbs chose to focus on the crime rate. It would be another three years before STRESS was completely eliminated with the arrival of Coleman Young as Detroit's first black mayor. A former auto worker and state senator, Young would later appoint the city's first black police chief, William Hart. With his strong union background, fiery personality, and determined style of leadership, he brought a new feeling of pride to the community. Young desegregated the police force and hired 700 new officers, but like Gribbs, he continued to struggle with the increasing rate of crime. Nevertheless, the masses found him appealing because of his tendency to shoot from the hip and tell the truth about the white man, as it pertained to the obstacles of dominance that made surviving a tough prospect for non-Caucasians. "When I see racism, I talk about it," Young was quoted as saying. "I've been doing that all my life and I hope I can stop talking about it. You know when that will happen? When I don't see any more racism." But with his forthright talk and aggressive approach to leadership, the mayor continued drawing scrutiny from federal officials, not unlike those who had tried to brand him a Communist two decades earlier. Any legal or ethical misstep in Young's administration might lead to the end of his political career or, if it got worse, his ability to remain a free man. Donnie, meanwhile, was embracing his freedom. STRESS would never have a reason, let alone a chance, to touch him if things continued in the direction they had begun. Once *Dopefiend* was published, his honeymoon commenced. "The Story of a Black Junkie," as it was subtitled, beat *Whoreson,* printed the following year, to the shelves. The ex-hustler was among the literati. Whether they liked it or not. Donnie had always envisioned himself achieving greatness, legitimate or otherwise, but he had no clue how much he would ultimately impact the world of urban publishing.

In the days that followed his first book's release, Donnie spent considerable time and energy brushing up on his vocabulary and polishing his image. It had never taken charm school to get him this far, but now he wanted to prepare for the attention that would accompany his newfound success. With what effort he could muster, he even managed to reduce his heroin use. He didn't pick up the "spike," as he named it, to stick in his arm, without the awareness that now he might have more to lose by indulging his habit. Just because he wrote *Dopefiend,* he didn't have to continue being one. He even took the bold step of becoming his own publicist. One afternoon, Donnie got himself together and made his way over to

479 Ledyard, the building that housed the *Michigan Chronicle*, right on the edge of downtown. The company had recently moved from Eliot, the same street where he'd attended Catholic school. A black-operated, weekly newspaper, it was headed by Longworth Quinn and had a proud history in the city. The *Chronicle* was a contemporary of two other influential organs that reported news and perspectives concerning people of color: the *Chicago Defender* and the *Pittsburgh Courier*.

Black journalism was undergoing a transformation, and not everyone thought it was for the better. Where, during the civil rights movement, such publications had played an active role in promoting change through keeping the community informed of victories and setbacks related to the struggle, by this time, many of the papers were becoming complacent. Without the ability to report on marches and demonstrations at the level of those that took place in the previous decade, the editors and staff writers tended to make black achievement and progress more of their focus. The result was a more narrow class orientation that highlighted business and professional men and women, leaving the masses, whose housing, economic, and educational opportunities had increased only marginally—if at all—excluded from coverage. Such fearless public statements as an early headline advising "When the Mob Comes and You Must Die, Take at Least One with You" attracted a dedicated and steady readership to the *Defender*. Its founder, Robert Sengstacke Abbott, had adopted his father's creed that "a good newspaper was one of the best instruments of service and one of the strongest weapons ever to be used in defense of a race which was deprived of its citizenship rights."

Similarly, the *Pittsburgh Courier* had developed a reputation for being in the vanguard of the black community. Like the *Defender*, it attracted a national audience, largely due to the broad scope of its reporting on current affairs. The paper was founded in 1910 by a small group of Pittsburgh's black residents at a time when the city's white-run publications ignored colored folks or relegated their coverage of these citizens primarily to crime and other lurid topics. The *Courier* utilized well-regarded writers, including Joel A. Rogers, whose "Your History" column discussed black achievements that commonly went unrecognized by the dominant social structure. The paper advocated for fair treatment of Negro servicemen during World War II, and by 1946, it produced fourteen local and national editions and had offices in twelve different cities.

Until the late 1950s, black newspapers thrived in virtually every major city. Then, as if activated by the yank of a chain, recognition of news value and potential readership connected with the civil rights movement flashed through the minds of the white media like a light bulb. Mainstream coverage led to a period of decline in the Negro press. With greater human, technological, and financial resources, the white papers and broadcast outlets could report a greater number of stories. A handful of the mainstream publications got hip to the advantage of having Negro staffers, who could get access to the neighborhoods and barbershops where white journalists would find resistance—or worse. But by 1955, only thirty-one black reporters were employed by the white media. Not until the '70s, when Donnie could have benefited from the exposure they might have provided, did the papers and TV stations actively recruit black talent. As Holloway House discovered not long before, however, in certain corners it was tough even to buy the attention they needed to promote their books. And while his face was still a handsome one, framed by his short, brown Afro and substantial mustache, or occasional goatee, Donnie was limited in his capacity for presentation. He was a decent communicator and his God-given charm never went away. Besides that, he was obviously no square. Donnie was more up on what was happening in the real world than probably anyone he knew. Yet, unlike Beck, he had never been to college or become particularly erudite on any philosophical subjects. His pitcher's arm had never suffered after all those years, and he had learned to play a good chess game, but Donnie wouldn't receive the interview requests and speaking invitations that his idol received. If he was going to get the media following that would help sell books, he'd better go after it himself.

Donnie walked into the *Chronicle* lobby unannounced and stopped at the front desk. He asked for Marie Teasley, a reporter whose byline he had followed enough to recognize her name. She kept track of the Detroit social scene, of which he could see himself becoming a part. A receptionist telephoned upstairs to the reporter as she worked in the newsroom.

"A young man is here to see you," the clerk said. "His name is Donald Goines."

The weather was warm that day, and it wasn't uncommon for visitors to stop in unannounced. In spite of its changing focus, the *Chronicle* was still regarded as a community institution. It was located one street over from Masonic Temple auditorium, around the corner from Cass Tech High and in the immediate vicinity of office buildings, so there was a fair amount of foot traffic and vehicle flow from the nearby Lodge Freeway. It was fairly convenient for anyone in the neighborhood, or working downtown, to stop in and pick up a newspaper or place a business ad. Marie watched Donnie as he walked the stairs to the second floor. She had heard his name before but didn't specifically place it. She thought she'd read about one or two of his crimes, though Donnie really hadn't raised the kind of hell that would legitimately earn him the title of newsmaker, hard as he may have tried. Nonetheless, Marie associated the uncommon Goines name with dicey dealings. It was certainly not one she heard in any of her professional circles.

"Are you Marie Teasley?" Donnie asked as they shook hands.

"Yes."

"I'm Donald."

She noticed that Donnie carried with him a couple of his books, but she had no inkling about why he was there at her office. Although she and columnist June Brown frequently had readers who popped in and asked to meet them, Donnie's introduction had a purpose behind it. Marie wrote a popular column called the "Jet Set." It highlighted the interests and achievements of people on the move. Anyone from a student at nearby Wayne State University to a party host might receive mention in the "Jet Set," depending on that particular week's news. The column was included in a ten-page lifestyle section that featured fashion, food, and entertainment, among other related topics. Donnie told her that he read the "Jet Set" and enjoyed it a great deal. Pleasantly surprised to hear him say he had become an author, Marie decided she would conduct an impromptu interview. They talked as Donnie sat by her desk.

The reporter was a little taken aback, however, when she saw the titles Donnie handed her.

"Oh, Lord," she thought to herself.

"Don't be alarmed," Donnie said, reading her thoughts. "I'm writing my life."

It was an unsolicited confession, and to a stranger. His new outlook allowed him a freedom he probably hadn't experienced in years. Marie flipped through the pages, immediately struck by Donnie's intimate knowledge of the subject matter they discussed. She asked how he wrote with such familiarity. Again, Donnie explained with complete honesty that it had all been a part of who he was since his boyhood in the North End of Detroit.

"But I'm coming through it," he proudly added.

Marie was impressed by the way Donnie handled himself. She would include him in her column. He never even had to make the formal pitch. Not much later, Marie was told about an assignment. Doris, a cousin on the Goines side of the family in New York, was so proud of Donnie's achievement that she wanted to put something together for him. She made her way to Michigan and threw Donnie a book-signing party. Relatives and friends gathered at a downtown hotel room where they lavished the man of the hour with praise. Donnie enjoyed all the attention. There were probably more congratulations offered there than he had received in all of his thirty-five years. Marie Teasley was among the well-wishers in attendance. She wrote an item for the paper and got a photograph of Donnie published along with it. Now thousands of people would know the name and face of Donald Goines. During that time, he actually managed the strength to lighten that monkey on his back and reduce his heroin consumption. For a moment, all too brief, it looked as if everything was coming together.

————

James Brown became known as the "hardest-working man in show business," but for dry cleaning, he couldn't come anywhere near touching Joe Goines. The family patriarch was still operating Northside at an amazing eighty-five years old when his son's first book was published. He had always been a little guy; however, those who learned about his bankroll during the years described him differently. Neighborhood folks often used the nickname "Big Joe." It had a glorious connotation, not unlike the "Big Chief " title he used in his occasional unwinding rituals, but it also revealed the esteem with which he was held. Men such as Joe and Shorty Hunt, who operated Hunt's Market, were essentially the backbone of the community. Their dedication to providing service was the sort that had helped keep black neighborhoods together. In truth, Joe had never hated the color; he just hated the hassles associated with blackness. And with the help of his wife, he had successfully raised and sheltered three children from a good many. Marie, Donnie, and Joan knew nothing of the terrifying, sanctioned racism that was everywhere when their parents grew up in the South, and they would never have to work for the white man as long as the family business remained. Still, they chose different routes.

For her part, Myrtle never failed to support her boy's vision of a successful literary career. She had no way of imagining that in the earliest stages of his becoming a popular author, Donnie would deeply wound her. In 1972, the entire world might as well have known what he thought of his mother with the introduction of two words: *whore son*. Despite her knowledge that the combined words formed the title of his second book for Holloway House, the detailed chronicle of events in the life of a Detroit prostitute's only child cut Myrtle to the core. *Whoreson: The Story of a Ghetto Pimp* sprang forth from Donnie's mind, not his upbringing. It was the product of both personal recollection and imagination. He really hadn't intended to publicly embarrass loved ones. Had not meant to make any particular commentary about his rearing at all, at least not on any conscious level. Donnie was simply doing what had gotten him a foot in the publisher's door—writing what he knew. Myrtle, however, wasn't anywhere close to thinking that way. This particular book, her boy had chosen to write in the first person. He had become the voice of Whoreson Jones, the story's bizarrely named central character. In Whoreson's words, Donnie told of how Jessie, a young, attractive woman who sells sex for a living, gave birth with the help of Big Mama, the boss of a tight prostitute stable in Black Bottom. Jessie has conceived the child with a Caucasian trick, who Whoreson will never know, leaving him with a beigelike hue that elicits the same hurtful nicknames Donnie was called as a boy. The plot is set in the same city, near some of the same neighborhoods and surroundings where the Goines family had been settled for going on forty years. But if these fact and fiction parallels weren't enough, there was the specific description of Whoreson's arrival into the world. No fanfare. No theatrics. Nothing even as compelling as the cutting of an umbilical cord. It was the season and the year of Whoreson's birth that begged to be read as autobiographical. Myrtle found it almost impossible not to wonder if she was actually the composite for this Jessie, about whom her son had written:

> *From what I have been told, it is easy to imagine the cold, bleak day when I was born into this world. It was December 10, 1940, and the snow had been falling continuously in Detroit all that day. The cars moved slowly up and down Hastings Street, turning the white flakes into slippery slush. Whenever a car stopped in the middle of the street, a prostitute would get out of it, or a whore would dart from one of the darkened doorways and get into the car. Jessie, a tall black woman, with high, narrow cheekbones, stepped from a trick's car, holding her stomach. Her dark, piercing eyes were flashing with anger. She began cursing the driver, using the vilest language imaginable about his parents and the nature of his birth.*

Donnie had placed Whoreson's birth date only five days and four years apart from his. True, Jessie bore no physical resemblance to his mother, but the book's other references were sufficient to hurt Myrtle's heart. Had she given Donnie any reason to see her as a whore? Was she somehow responsible for his poor choices? Donnie and his sisters labored to convince her that the thoughts and observations in the book belonged completely to a fictional character, though they never believed she fully accepted the explanation. After all, the facts remained: Donnie had run away from her to Korea and returned a different person. A man-child in a not-so-promising land. Was there something more his mother could have done to show him a better means of making his way through this world? It would be several books later before he acknowledged Myrtle in the same public way; this time there would be no confusion about his message. He thanked her on a dedication page, writing ". . . to my mother, Myrtle Goines, who had confidence in my writing ability."

Black Gangster reached book racks by summer, the same year as *Whoreson*. Donnie was at the start of a creative torrent that wouldn't slow down any time soon. Overall, it didn't take much for him to come up with a scenario in the vein of what he had already sold to Holloway House. He had plenty of those. The mechanics of the storytelling could always be worked out with his writing coaches on the West Coast. Donnie located a character named Prince at the center of *Black Gangster*. In the opening pages, Prince is being let out of his cell at Jackson as he and other prisoners are led to the mess hall. Suggesting the author's familiarity with the history of the old-time Detroit mobsters, such as those in the Purples and the Little Navy Gang, Donnie brought Prince out of the pen and up through the ranks of the underground as a bootlegger. Finally, the character finds himself as the powerful boss of organized crime. Like *Dopefiend,* it would become an urban classic. Donnie had finally matured to the point that Prince's ascension no longer resembled his personal aspirations. There was, however, a personal aspiration he held outside of his writing career, one he'd held for many years: to kick. To kick, or break the addiction, was, in fact, the most deeply held desire of many an addict. It was true that he'd done terrible things, undoubtedly contributed tears and heartache to the lives of others. At various times, he had even been deemed unfit to exist as a human being outside of the strictest twenty-four-hour supervision. Donnie knew within himself that no person who was controlled by any source was fit to be called anything except a slave. Perhaps the most torturous form of slavery was the one that had complicity at its root. The kind that felt like hell to let go. He was tired of heroin's torture. Had been since that first time he asked his mother to lock him in the bedroom. However tired he was, though, he wasn't ready to sign himself over to the whitecoats. A rehab clinic or hospital was more than he felt ready to deal with. Maybe the concept of confinement and restrictions seemed too much like prison.

Marie was now married to her third husband, a career military man named Warren Richardson. She and her clan, including Charles, who had become a free-spirited young performer, settled in an area of Georgia where Richardson was stationed. The community of Warner Robins was about 120 miles south of Atlanta. Located in the central region of the state, it was relatively small in size with a population of about 30,000. Marie had become accustomed to traveling the country and relocating when necessary. Her children would total four, with the birth of Jean, a daughter. Detroit virtually became a second home in the time and space that separated them from the city. As Donnie continued adjusting to his new professional direction, he decided that a change of scenery was in order. He gathered his belongings and headed south to spend time with his sister and her family. Donnie would use the time in Warner Robins to continue his writing but also to try and distance himself from familiar temptations. With Joe and Myrtle slowing down and Joan tending after her own clan, he could use a support network, and he hadn't spent a great deal of time with his big sister in recent years. Meanwhile, the nephew he'd spent the most time and energy trying to coax—or corrupt—into manhood had developed a talent for music. Charles could sing and play drums. He began writing songs and preparing for what he hoped would be a career of making records and grooving on the stage. His bands performed as Round House, Free Soil, and Doc Holliday. They played rock and blasted southern blues. It was rare for a drummer to handle lead vocals, but Charles could melt soul into the microphone. Like much of his generation, he was heavily influenced by the Motown Sound. He grew to love Marvin Gaye. Yet, Charles was versatile enough to sing like a white boy when the music called for it. He began to dress and adapt himself to the part of universal rock rebel, in the young and free tradition of a long line that preceded him. And like a long line of musicians' mothers before her, Marie was less than thrilled. She knew of her son's talent, but the accoutrements daunted her. Heels and pouches had somehow never fit in with the image she had envisioned for her oldest boy, no matter what his career choice.

It was cool for Charles to be able to reconnect with his uncle. To whatever extent that he had become hip or street wise, it was not without Donnie's influence. Charles remembered the way he'd walk the neighborhood in Detroit when he was younger, without fear of a hassle from anyone. His uncle's reputation had its benefits as a hedge of protection that followed him when he went to buy a candy bar. At the same time, he could recall occasions when he didn't know what in the world could be wrong with Donnie, like when old Joe gathered the power from somewhere and shoved Donnie across the room. In a drugged-out haze, Donnie was feeling ornery and Joe didn't appreciate the mistreatment he saw being given to his grandson, Charles. Donnie could play the crazy nigger out in the world; Joe wasn't going to abide it in his presence. Whether it was for the good or bad, Charles knew few dull moments when Donnie was around. Now he would have the opportunity to see his uncle in the flesh again. Unbeknownst to Charles, it would also be the last occasion during which they spent any substantial amount of time together. For now, it appeared to be a good period, and there appeared to be favorable circumstances for Donnie to beat his drug habit. He met and hung out with his nephew's bandmates. He had plenty of stories to tell and a truckload of shit to talk about everything from war to women. At the same time, he continued to focus on his work, mentioning that he'd like to attend a book conference out West. Donnie seemed genuinely content with his stay when, as quickly as he arrived, he decided to leave. Charles wasn't sure how much the stay had accomplished, but he knew he had seen no indication that Donnie was shooting up. That wasn't testimony Charles had been able to offer on many occasions.

Jessie and Nancy Sailor were established Detroiters who had moved north from Georgia. Jessie did well as a company man with Ford Motor. His cousin, Earl Little, had done quite the opposite. While living near Lansing, about ninety miles from Detroit, Earl was killed in 1931, reportedly by the Black Legion, a white supremacist group. While he had been a Baptist minister, he was also part of a worldwide movement organizing for Marcus Garvey's influential Universal Negro Improvement Association. In time, the white folks in the community came to regard Reverend Little as an agitator. Much later, his seventh son, Malcolm, would become even more widely known for his efforts to awaken the masses as the Nation of Islam's spokesman, Malcolm X. Jessie and Nancy had children of their own, fifteen in all. They resembled a big southern family living in the city. The second-youngest child was a daughter named Shirley Ann. Acknowledged as a striking beauty, with brown skin and delicate features, by the time she reached womanhood she had strayed from the path her folks had laid out for her and her siblings to follow. Shirley hooked up with a pimp who eventually turned her out. When their relationship ended, she moved on. By the time she met Donnie, Shirley had a son and a daughter. Though she had developed a level of street knowledge, Shirley had a childish innocence, a sweetness, about her. The combination of her physical and character attributes was enough to quickly gain Donnie's attention. Shirley was ten years younger than him, yet they connected as a couple. She grew to love Donnie dearly and deeply. They appeared to complement one another well. Close to Joanie in age, Shirley found approval in the Goines family. And she was enough of a fox that she didn't ever have to worry about Joe slamming a door in her face.

Donnie, Shirley, and her children settled into a place together. It was probably the most domestic setup he had experienced in his entire adulthood, but he seemed OK with it. After all, he had done plenty out in the world, and he was still a fairly young man. For better or worse, he had made his own way for the past twenty years. So with his new career, it was appropriate that he adapt a new lifestyle. His common-law wife, Shirley would be about as close as he'd ultimately come to having a bride. Their daughter, Donna, named in unmistakable similarity to her father, was born to complete the household. She became a Sailor, rather than a Goines. In the meantime, other Sailors had begun moving west from Detroit. Shirley had siblings in California, which was, just by coincidence, where Donnie's business contacts were based. The couple agreed that they would try something new together: living in Los Angeles.

At one point, Donnie had made his way out there before, appearing as an extra in the film *Soylent Green,* which reached theaters in the seventies. Set in 2022, it was a sci-fi flick starring Charlton Heston. He played a cop named Thorn, who uncovered the chilling source of a government-manufactured food after investigating a murder. Donnie's screen time in the film was nothing worth mentioning, but the experience probably contributed to the final motivating factor in his decision to relocate: Donnie wanted to see at least one of his books become a movie. His work would have been a good fit for theaters, with the recent arrival of what the trade publication *Variety* dubbed "blaxploitation" flicks. A combination of the words *black* and *exploitation,* the phrase described works that largely depicted characters in stereotypical images but who often operated entirely outside of the social order. Hundreds of derelict, downtown-area theaters in urban cities beckoned these releases and the audiences who would pay admission to appreciate them. *Sweet Sweetback's Baadasssss Song,* which opened in 1971, was described by the *Los Angeles Times* as "a series of earthy vignettes, where [director Mario] Van Peebles evokes the vitality, humor, pain, despair and omnipresent fear that is life for so many African Americans." Along with *Shaft* and 1972's *Superfly,* the release helped open the door to an era of story lines in which, through whatever means, the black characters would win in the end.

This time, Donnie's trip to the West Coast would have greater longevity and more sense of purpose. He who hesitated was lost, and Donnie no longer felt lost in his goals. Again, he told friends he wanted to kick; the trip to Georgia hadn't done it for him as he'd hoped. They chipped in to help him do what he felt led to do. The day when he and Shirley prepared to fly out of Detroit was one to remember. Donnie must have decided he would need to show Los Angeles that Detroit was hip to fashion because he threw on a suit and a sharp, wide-brimmed hat resembling the popular style that had been worn in *Superfly*. And sexy Shirley was looking the part as Donnie's woman: A red mini dress and thigh-high boots that she wore the hell out of made up her ensemble. The family saw them off at the airport. They knew this could be a flight into what might become Donnie's most life-changing success yet.

Los Angeles had seen its share of devastation in the black community. Two years before Detroit caught fire behind the police raid, residents in the South Central neighborhood of Watts participated in the first major race-related uprising of the 1960s. A twenty-one-year-old man was arrested that August, after a cop flagged down his vehicle on suspicion of intoxication. Not unlike the scene outside the after-hours joint in Detroit, a crowd of observers taunted the officer, and so a second cop was called to the scene. As elsewhere in the nation, the air had already grown thick with racial stress, not to mention a late-summer heat wave. There was good reason for those in depressed neighborhoods to be tense. Black folks numbered around half a million by that time, but with the western emigration, much like the northern movement, plenty found themselves out of work and living in overcrowded ghetto sections. In another unfortunate parallel with the urban centers elsewhere, L.A. cops had begun to develop a reputation for brutality that would linger in their ranks for many years. Eyewitnesses said it was the second officer who became overly aggressive when he showed up to assist with the suspected drunk driver. The cop swung his baton at members of the crowd, unnecessarily, they said. Soon, news of the altercation spread through the streets and alleys of South Central, leading to violence on a massive scale. During the rebellion, there were four days of burning, looting, and wreaking wholesale havoc, then another three days of sporadic outbreaks as an estimated 35,000 people participated. The toll, after a combined effort of city, county, and National Guard members to end the disturbance, was thirty-four dead—all but three black—at least a thousand wounded, 4,000 arrested, and $200 million in property damage. It all began only five days after the Voting Rights Act was signed. Proof that symbolic legislation was no substitute for treating men and women with dignity.

Los Angeles city administrators first tried to pin the blame for the eruption on outside agitators. There was no discontent among the good Negroes of Watts, they contended. Later information, however, revealed that most of those involved with the rebellion had lived there their entire lives. The rage they expressed had been set off by police but had grown as a manifestation of their resentment of Caucasian shopkeepers in the neighborhood, another element in a relationship with the black community that would remain contentious long after the last ashes had lost their glow. It was not by mistake or coincidence that black churches, neighborhood libraries, businesses, and homes were virtually untouched. The destruction was actually applauded in circles containing those who saw it as a necessary signal to the powers-that-were. It helped to define political camps in the next phase of social struggle, though the community never completely recovered. And the fallout was more far-reaching than the boundaries of Watts: A number of political careers were damaged, including that of Edmund G. "Pat" Brown, the liberal governor, who was assigned his share of the blame by conservative politicians. It was to become a tired and pitiful, yet recurring, scenario. Wherever black men and women lived in unofficially segregated, so-called inner-city areas, there loomed the likelihood that one form of head game or another would be played—with white insecurity as a primary rule.

Things hadn't always been quite as bad for people of color in L.A. As far back as the turn of the century, the city was becoming a multicultural destination. Caucasians and those of African descent found themselves in the midst of a much broader ethnic makeup. The city's Spanish roots, combined with its relative proximity to

Asia, made it attractive to Mexicans, Chinese, and Japanese. While black folks dealt all alone with white hatred in other regions of the country, here it was the newer citizens who often found themselves sharing the brunt of the pain. Competition between the cultures for opportunities added an element of difficulty that was largely unfamiliar to the experience of folk with common heritage. Negroes who discovered life on the West Coast and migrated early on often found what they'd been looking for. Between 1900 and 1920, there was relative prosperity. About 36 percent of the black population owned private homes, compared with just 11 percent in New Orleans and less than 3 percent in New York. Black-operated businesses popped up along Central Avenue downtown, and in 1903 businessman Theodore Troy set up the Los Angeles Forum, an agency designed to direct community growth and help black migrants in their transition. Forum members helped train others in the conduct that increased Caucasian tolerance, as whites tried to contain growth of the ghetto territory that formed around the Central Avenue Hotel.

Though black folks inhabited various L.A. neighborhoods earlier on, housing covenants eventually pressed them out of white residential areas. By 1930, the city's vast majority of Negroes were located in the overcrowded community of South Central. They were largely relegated to domestic and service jobs. But like Detroit's Black Bottom, the Avenue area developed into a place that became known for its nightlife, drawing comparisons to Harlem on the East Coast, and was home to churches, restaurants, and other businesses. Politically, there were also black leaders who emerged from the consolidation of the constituency. Supported by the large numbers of Negro voters in their district, officials like state assemblymen Frederick Roberts and Augustus Hawkins enjoyed long careers in government. As of 1940, the city ranked as America's fifth-largest, with about 1.5 million residents. In fewer than 100 years of existence, Los Angeles had grown more rapidly than most of the other municipalities in the nation.

Along with black residents, Asian and Mexican immigrants had contributed to the increase. In 1943, around the time when young men began sporting the flashy, oversized zoot suits as they walked the streets, they managed to attract the wrong sort of attention. The ensemble had become popular among Negroes, largely because of its association with jazz culture. Mexican fellows picked up the trend, fashioning their hair into ducktails to complete their slick, head-to-toe look. Zoots were considered luxury items at a time when fabric was being rationed for the war effort and were often worn for special occasions like birthday parties or dances. Their wearers might be heading into downtown L.A. to the Million Dollar Theater on Third and Broadway, or the Orpheum Theater between Eighth and Ninth, where the big bands showed up. They occasionally crossed paths with servicemen, who checked out the penny arcades where ladies worked the bar. Or they might amble down to Main Street to enjoy a burlesque show. The zoot owners, who proudly wore their hipster suits like knights in the armor of defiance, were negatively portrayed in the media. Newspapers often presented them as hoodlums in articles printed close to the latest war coverage. Perhaps that was what provoked white soldiers and sailors to physically assault the colorfully attired blacks and Mexicans without provocation. The ensuing clashes would become known as the Zoot Suit Riots. They started just about two weeks before similar hell broke loose on Detroit's Belle Isle. A June 9, 1943, article in the *Los Angeles Examiner* offered a look into the peculiar conflict:

> . . . Harold Tabor, 32, Long Beach sailor, was severely beaten by a gang of zooters at 103rd and Graham St. He suffered a broken nose, serious facial cuts. He told officers at Georgia St. hospital that he had been visiting his sister, Dorothy Edmonson, 1133 East 103rd St.
>
> "I was passing a pool hall en route to a grocery store when the gang hopped me," he said.
>
> George Lorigo, 19, was arrested on a charge of battery after Tabor's beating. The sailor was later transferred to Long Beach naval hospital for X-ray examination.
>
> Two soldiers and a Negro zoot suiter were taken into custody after

a riot at the corner of Second and Spring Sts. And police, cruising throughout the city in scouting forays, dispersed mobs, hunted for others. Police ordered groups of more than three to "break it up" everywhere in the downtown area, and the presence of armed officers on every street resembled martial law rule. Two officers were stationed on every corner of Main, Spring and Broadway, between First St. and Pico Blvd. Two more officers were in the center of each block.

Squads of riot breakers, packed 18 in a truck, roamed the city, investigated mob reports, arrested suspects. Traffic on Main St. was bumper to bumper, moving slowly as city officials tried [sic] to solve the zoot suit problem.

Navy shore patrol officers and Bagley army military police added to the martial law resemblance. They walked in and out of bars, dancehalls, drug stores, bus stations. They kept servicemen on the move, asked for proof of leaves and liberties.

One of the most serious outbreaks of terrorism occurred in Watts. There, three PE trains were stoned. At least three passengers were injured by shattered glass windows . . . Gangsterism in Watts continued into the early hours of today. Twelve Negroes ambushed a 17-year-old white high school student, asked him if he was a "zoot suiter" and when he said "no," the fight started. The victim, Joe M. Steddum of 8834 Banders St., Watts, received a five-inch cut on his left forehead, requiring six stitches at the emergency hospital, 3060 Slauson St., to mend.

Police took Daniel Malone into custody at Sixth and Main Sts. when they discovered a long club hidden down his pants leg.

Servicemen continued to roam the city's streets through all this hectic night despite the "out of bounds" order issued at 3:15 yesterday afternoon. It came from Rear Adm. D. W. Bagley, a commandant of the 11th Naval district in San Diego, and addressed to all activities, it read: "Until further notice, except for special occasions approved by the commanding officer, the city of Los Angeles will be out of bounds for all enlisted personnel of the naval services not attached to the stations within this city, or in travel status. Activities located in the city of Los Angeles will, except in special cases, grant liberty to married men or those subsisted off stations."

Augmented police forces continued their roundup of riot suspects, meanwhile. Arrests of zoot suiters were reported in all sections of the county . . . But zoot suit panty gangs of hoodlums
continued to lose their trousers to servicemen, and in many cases
nearly lost what was in 'em.

The slanted coverage continued, often depicting zoots as the ag-
gressors. Largely in response to the episodes, a multiracial coali-
tion was formed among Mexican and Negro activists. This alliance
included newly formed special-interest groups that joined in the
effort to prevent additional violence against the zoots. They also
protested job discrimination and assisted Japanese in America as
they relocated from confinement camps. The cultural aesthetic of
L.A. had changed, of course, by the 1970s. Though it was still a
multicultural mecca, long hair, halter tops, and bell bottoms were
among universally popular choices in fashion. When Donnie and
Shirley arrived in Los Angeles, they settled in the Western Avenue
area, composed of mainly apartments and some individual home
dwellings.

With his lady along, Donnie met with Bentley Morriss at the
Holloway House office. He struck the publisher as being very different from the type of material he submitted. Donnie was quiet
and unassuming, with no outward resemblance to the characters
he crafted. Morriss found Donnie pliable and receptive. Holloway
House bought Donnie an electric typewriter. They knew he wrote
longhand, and without Joanie available to provide her services,
making his work presentable for publication would be a big hassle
if he weren't handed the proper tools. Knowing that he was still
fairly new to the game, the editors handled Donnie with care.
They would discuss things like scene-setting and how to flesh out
his stories. There had been no contractual stipulation about the
number of books Donnie was to write. Needing the money, he
would simply say something like, "I've got an idea . . ." and the process would begin. They never required an outline. Now and then,
Donnie would head over to 8060, and he and Morriss would go to
lunch together. As Morriss had cultivated a relationship with Iceberg

Slim, he liked to believe that he and Donnie eventually became friends.

Shirley came across as a supportive and devoted partner. When she got the opportunity, she would often share her concern about Donnie with his newfound colleagues in the business. L.A. had its own smack connections, and, in spite of his efforts, it didn't seem to take long before Donnie discovered them. Unlike any number of addicts who would drift off into oblivion after injecting themselves with heroin, Donnie would generally nod out for a couple of minutes, then wake up and immediately find his way to the typewriter. Wong had become like medication; its high, the equivalent of relief from a severe illness. Drugs still had a hold on him, and, with added stress, all he could do was continue to fight. With the cost of his habit added to their combined budget, money became tight for Donnie and Shirley. Every now and then, he would do something that reflected a lapse in judgment. As had been his way for a good while, he liked to gamble on occasion. At least once, he traveled from L.A. to Las Vegas. For whatever changes he made in his conduct, Donnie never quite shed that hustler mentality. He continued hoping for the big payoff. And so far, books didn't appear to be the means by which he could expect to receive it. But things didn't go well during the Nevada trip. Donnie blew all his shit. It hadn't been the same as playing cards and shooting craps the way he did as an adolescent. Folks in Vegas were unsympathetic. Holloway House had to bail him out. Back in L.A., Bentley Morriss pondered the writer's missteps and problems. Donnie seemed to have a constant affinity for drawing tragedy to his life. As a result, Holloway House was constantly faced with the possibility of receiving that desperate and unexpected phone call. Morriss accepted the trade-off of occasional trouble in exchange for the author's talent. In the end, it was a choice he wouldn't regret.

Conversely, Donnie had already been having misgivings about his relationship with the publisher. It may have been irrational, but he felt the company wasn't supporting him enough. One neatly typed, undated letter to an unidentified publishing house representative, or perhaps written as a general query, revealed his thoughts:

Sir,

I am trying to find a publisher who might be interested in handling my work. At this time, I have twelve novels on the market. As
far as sales are concerned, I think they are selling quite well.

He stated that his two best novels, *Whoreson* and *Dopefiend*,
were each approaching 100,000—*Whoreson* at 80,753; *Dopefiend*
at 88,276 copies sold. The third fastest moving, he wrote, was *Black
Gangster*, with 45,652. Out of either a watchful paranoia or a seldom
displayed business sense, Donnie had checked on the figures.

Now what I am interested in is getting a better contract. I won't
mention what I'm getting now, but you more than likely have a very
good idea of what I'm knocking down. If you are interested in doing business with me, please write and let me know how much you
would be willing to pay. If we can come to terms, I'll send you a
novel in about a month.
Sincerely, Donald Goines

He signed in pen but never sent the original. More curiously, despite the fact that he chose to relocate, it listed 17186 Maine as the
return address, suggesting that it was written before he ever left
Detroit. But the market for black readership wouldn't have provided him with many other options, and Holloway House was
pleased with his progress. Where the book sales were concerned,
there appeared few reasons for them not to be. Still, they knew
there was another issue. On a day when Donnie and Shirley showed
up at the office together, Bentley Morriss thought he would try his
hand at intervention. When Shirley excused herself, he pulled Donnie's coat about the heroin problem.

"Look," he started. "I'm not a saint and I'm not a psychologist,
but I think what you're doing, Donald, is not good for you."

Donnie always behaved like a perfect gentleman in their meetings. He wasn't rude at all with his response.

"I've got it under control," he said. But he lied. He hadn't managed to truly get it under control since the first time he encountered

smack. There remained, however, an entirely different element that Donnie found even more impossible to manipulate in his favor. Befitting its tradition, the LAPD remained an oppressive presence in the community. Having been a criminal, it was fair to say Donnie had developed a natural aversion to police officers. But there was something about this particular element of cop that seemed more hateful to him. These cops didn't even know who the hell he was. His frequent drug possession notwithstanding, he hadn't committed the types of crime that attracted most of the attention he received from police back home. It seemed that Los Angeles officers fucked with him simply because they could. Combined with the money trouble, it was all beginning to be too much for him. He vented his frustrations into the typewriter. This time, there was no fiction in any of the words. Across the top of the first page, Donnie scribbled "Private Thoughts on a Lonely Sunday, Sept. 1, 1973":

This is just a brief account on this Sunday afternoon . . . To awaken broke, without enough money to buy smokes is a feeling that I [know]. To awaken without enough money to buy cigarettes is just about rock bottom, which is a form of life that I can't ever seem to overcome. I have been poor so long that its become sickening. Today, I fussed with my woman over ten dollars; I needed the money to get a fix so that I could type. True, I really need a fix to be able to write. If I don't fix, my mind comes to a standstill. The only thing I can think about is, "Where and how can I get a fix?"

Donnie's reflections revealed the degree to which he had begun recognizing his addiction's impact on his burgeoning career.

Without drugs, at this stage of my life, [it's] not only difficult, but damn near impossible. I can't concentrate enough to work without them. If I smoke weed, it makes me daydream too much, so that in the end, I don't have any work did. If I get a shot of heroin, I'm able to work from morning to night, my writing seems to be better, and I can think.

Confessing such a dependency that he couldn't function without drugs, the pensive writer allowed that medical attention was likely the answer.

> *In need to go into a hospital or something because I'm not able to afford the price of drugs now. I don't want to start back to stealing; I'm having enough trouble with the courts now, so I don't do any hustling whatsoever. The only money we have to live on is the fifty-dollar check I get from my publisher once a week, plus Shirley's check, which comes every two weeks. It's a hell of a small amount . . .*

Along with penury, he wrote of other sources of daily stress. The sentiment ranged from sarcasm to anguish, at times distorting the lines between fantasy, reality, and a junkie's fuzzy perception of both. Of his desire not to worry "about the police harassing me whenever I decided to go down the street to the store":

> *Now I realize if I were white, this wouldn't be such a problem, because my publishers could then give me the keys to one of their homes abroad and tell me to just keep the place together without misusing it. But, being of the black race, there is always the chance that we will contaminate whatever we touch, so I understand . . . but why, why refuse me the opportunity to do so much for so little? Even if it cost you five thousand dollars out of your private account to send me somewhere that I can work uninterrupted for just four to six months—not on garbage—but on one book that might not be a number one best seller, but it would be the best that I'd ever do.*

Donnie's thoughts appear to have occurred almost randomly, as he questioned his worth, perhaps not just to the company that contracted him:

> *Now let's try another tack. If my life were in the balance, would Holloway House think I was worth this much money if someone had demanded that much money for my return?*

And then he seemed to jerk himself into coherency, appearing every bit the concerned and rational author.

> *I don't want to sound [d]efiant, or like some smart-ass nigger. What I'm trying to say is, "Help." . . . I want to write, but there is not much money in paperbacks, as we both know, unless the writer turns them out like comic books. But I want to write something that you and I would both be proud of. I have the novel in mind, but it's utterly impossible for me to spend that much time on one book when I can turn out three others in the same length of time.*

Donnie continued, directing his concerns to the typewriter as if they might be vicariously addressed:

> *By this time, you are wondering, "Where is this letter going?" and how can you possibl[y] help, I hope.*

Urging would-be benefactors to take a risk on him, he elaborated.

> *This is my answer—take a gamble. Am I asking too much? Would it really hurt you for you and Ralph to sit down and figure out some way to help me? Does your magazine need a writer in Africa, or anywhere other than right here in Los Angeles? I mean is it utterly impossible for you to see how in helping me, that you might just help yourself?*

At stake was not only his future with Holloway House, but his future as a stable, secure individual and family provider. Donnie continued acting as his own best advocate, urging an imaginary audience to recognize his good work and potential, if not *"destroyed by this system that we live under."* As if he were stalked prey, Donnie expressed feeling "like a bird whos[e] [sic] wings have been clipped." Moving to another home in Los Angeles wouldn't be enough.

> *I'm still afraid to go out the door to the store unless I'm carrying two children with me. It's too much. My sanity is slowly going. I see*

it coming—what the black ghettoes couldn't do, Los Angeles is slowly doing.

Apparently, on occasion, urgent thoughts of crime had even returned, but Donnie resisted.

I don't want another case, so I live like this, looking forward to Friday so that I can at least have the fun of driving out to Melrose, even though I bring my family along then, not taking any chances.

If nothing else, do this much for me: Check the paper work and see if I have enough money coming so that you can ship me and my family back to Mich. There, I can at least live free.

Donnie had become so frantic to get out of the "concentration camp" which was his existence that he would sacrifice four months' prepaid rent in favor of Detroit's approaching winter climate.

I don't even have coats for me or my children, but I'd rather die of freezing than stay here and lose my mind. Maybe I have been rambling in this letter, but I hope you understand one thing. The police have won. I can't cope with them much longer.

Then, not unlike what might have occurred if he had fallen into a sudden nod, the words faded.

I have never hated white, but since being here, this city has made me hate everything in a . . .

Blank space, in the place of characters, filled the remainder of the last line. "Private Thoughts" ended abruptly, having apparently failed to reach its conclusion. For whatever Donnie's intentions with the letter, there was no clear manifestation of its impact beyond the mental and emotional release it provided. Whether he had seriously considered sending it to Bentley Morriss and Ralph Weinstock or to any other professional contacts versus merely rehearsing what he might get up the nerve to express to them, it was a libation of his soul that he had poured out onto the paper. Although it was filled with typographical and spelling errors, the message contained in "Private Thoughts" could not be misunderstood. Double-spaced and bearing the name "Goines," manuscript-style in the upper-left-hand corner, they were three pages of desperation. Gone was the arrogance he injected into the dialogue of his most brash-talking characters. In its place was the naked fear and insecurity of a creative yet frazzled mind. The pages would be retired to his personal briefcase and discovered more than a year after the date when he typed them. In another retrospective moment, he never chose to bother with the typewriter. Donnie got into the habit of scrawling thoughts onto paper, these written after what were the apparent beginnings of some rewrite work on a novel. Beneath the words "Page 73–74 Rape Scene," he printed: "Can't get it right. Damn [it's] hot here. Can't stand it here. When my check gets here we're going to Detroit."

Prodigal Son

*. . . I turned on my heel and departed, on my way to pick up my
new Cadillac. And then from there, I'd hit the highway. Like I said,
Los Angeles and me had had enough of each other . . . After all, I've
been out here for damn near five years. It's time I slowed down.
Maybe now I can settle down and live respectably. Something I've
been wanting to do all my life."*

—Never Die Alone, Donald Goines

If things were going to get any better for Donnie, Shirley, and the
children in California, there obviously wasn't much indication of it.
Donnie had failed to establish any significant contacts in the film
industry. Failed to kick. Failed to get any real sense of refuge whatsoever. All he really had to show for his time in Los Angeles that
suggested any sense of achievement was a black Cadillac with
a white convertible top. He had never bought one when he was
a pimp. Now, at least, he could say he drove a nice ride. There was
no doubt that he wanted to put it on the highway as soon as possible. He continued that stream-of-consciousness method of jour-
naling that he did from time to time, summarizing in a checklist his
need to depart California. "Spoke to my Mama today, she said
come home now—Joan to[o]. Received $250.00 from Wea Wea;
she sent a large box of food—heavy—cost a fortune to send. Have
to get out of here . . . to get wong—Shirley wants to go home to[o].
Feels like I'm losing it—not enough time. We are leaving today.
Got my check and money Wea Wea sen[t]." The folks at Holloway
House didn't seem entirely surprised that Donnie was going home.

It had been months, but less than a year. His peace and sanity were on far shakier ground than they had been the day he arrived. If he could get back on familiar concrete, he figured, at least he couldn't do any worse.

Following the 3,000-mile drive home, Donnie was slow to make contact with the friends who had chipped in to send him away. It wasn't long, however, before phones were ringing. "Did he call you yet? He's back." Walter shook his head and laughed at the news of his old friend's return. He wasn't angry, at least not in any way that a good cussin' out wouldn't cover. Donnie was trying to find his way, and through it all he still had people who believed in him. He and Shirley found a place to live in Highland Park, where they planned to readjust to the slower pace they had begun missing. Before the close of 1973, he had added *Street Players*, the story of Earl "The Pearl," a pimp who sits on top of the world until fate and karma pay him a visit, to his body of literary work. He was gaining name recognition. The work that followed in July was *White Man's Justice, Black Man's Grief*, which he dedicated to Shirley. Her "love and infinite patience helped me to keep the faith and to make my editorial deadline . . ." Donnie explained. He acknowledged a few personal supporters in the family of acquaintances Charles and Carol Cunningham, then, in yet another conflicting sentiment, added the folks at Holloway House: "and for my publisher and editor, whose help and kindness I doubt I'll ever be able to repay in full." But that last sentiment would change. Donnie had intended *White Man's Justice, Black Man's Burden* as the title, but in the final draft, *Grief* is what made it to the cover. Drawing from his experiences in and out of the joint, it was written almost like an exposé of the court and prison systems. Fiction was merely the weapon of choice for the truths Donnie told in revealing the fucked-up conditions of the overcrowded, dirty, and often-violent jail facilities that housed the innocent-until-proven-guilty in urban communities.

In an uncharacteristic move, Donnie wrote a forthright and personal author's note in the book's opening pages:

Since this work of fiction deals with the court system, I'd like to direct the reader's attention to an awesome abuse inflicted daily upon the less fortunate—the poor people of this country—an abuse which no statesman, judge or attorney (to my knowledge) has moved to effectively remedy. I'm speaking of the bail-bond system.

He reported the county jails' daily herding of poor blacks and whites. Donnie witnessed it numerous occasions while incarcerated, and he pointed out that many of those eventually found innocent could spend more than a year locked away, "simply because they couldn't raise bail-bond money." Removing himself from such scenarios, he told of the stunning injustice, through which "those who are lucky enough to raise bail-bond money will never get it back—even if their cases are eventually thrown out of court, or if they are tried and found innocent!"

Donnie went on in measured written tones, drawing a link between the system's flaws and economic hardships.

Because of the overzealousness or stupidity or (and let's be honest) bigotry of some law enforcement officers, countless numbers of poor persons have to pawn their belongings, sell their cars or borrow money from finance companies (another high-interest bill they can't afford) to regain their freedom so that they can, hopefully, stay gainfully employed, only to be found not guilty as charged when their cases come up in court. . . . The cities should be made to reimburse those falsely accused. . . . Then and only then would the cities' taxpayers exert pressure at the upper levels, forcing policemen to use better judgment than to arrest people on ridiculous Catch-22 charges that they know will be thrown out of court. Black people are aware of this abuse, for a disproportionate number of blacks suffer from it constantly. But black people are powerless to remedy the situation. . . . Make no mistake about it, there's big money in the bail bond business, and most of it is being made at the expense of poor blacks.

Printed at the end of the statement:—Donald Goines, 1973. From somewhere between the editing staff and Donnie came the label "An Angry Preface," which was used as a heading for the introduction. It had the ring of white folks' translation. Whether Donnie or an editor was responsible, the heading took away from the thoughtfulness of the short essay. In actuality, Donnie's tone revealed no anger of any kind. It was a simply stated yet well-argued position that reflected careful analysis, not emotion. Rare indeed, though, was the occasion when a black man or woman could speak boldly in condemnation of some condition that affected people of color and not be accused of anger, no matter how calm he or she really was. Perhaps ironically, calmness and composure were major attributes in the man Donnie created as the main character for *White Man's Justice, Black Man's Grief*. Fitting with the routine he developed, he had sketched out Chester's composite, along with the composites of the other men he would encounter during his extended stay in Detroit's Wayne County Jail:

> Chester Hines—Tall, slim, brown-skinned, in his early thirties, doing time for possession of pistol, 3–5 years; Willie Brown—Twenty-four years old, short, black and husky, doing time for B-E . . . gets out before Chester's time is up; Charles Williams—Willie's rap partner . . . Tall build, husky, plays on football team, boxes inside prison; Albert Jones—Doing life in prison for killing girlfriend, brown-complexioned, fat, eats all the time, teacher in the prison's school; Billy Johnson—23 years old, short, black with large gut from eating prison meals . . . been in prison since he was 17 . . .

Interesting as Donnie's brief sketches may have been, not all of the characters made *White Man's Justice, Black Man's Grief* in the final edit. The book really didn't have much of a plot but centered mostly on its protagonist, his experiences and observations. If it wasn't Donnie's way of offering a literary tribute, it was an uncanny coincidence that he called the man Chester Hines. Author Chester Himes had long left the country to live out his days in Europe by the time Holloway first began publishing Donnie's work. Himes's black crime and detective novels were often set in Harlem, just as Donnie placed so many of his ghetto dramas in Detroit. Himes was really a father figure in the urban fiction genre. But that's not where the similarities between Himes and Donnie, or Himes and Chester Hines, the similarly named character, ended. Himes was released from the Ohio State Penitentiary the same year Donnie was born. Like Donnie, he was born one of three children to relatively well-off parents. And, like Donnie, he left school, though he had performed well up until his first year of college, and became involved with drugs and petty crime. Cleveland, Ohio, only a couple of hours from Detroit, became Himes's stomping grounds. As a young man, he was convicted—much like Donnie—of armed robbery. The authors also shared the environment of prison cells as the backdrops in which they began to develop their writing. As Donnie would eventually, Himes traveled to Los Angeles, where he had hoped to parlay his craft into a film career. When he learned that none of the studios were interested in a Negro writer, however, he sought other work in California, leading to experiences that helped inspire his first two published books. But lack of critical and commercial attention for his work contributed to his decision to expatriate. In Paris, he joined a community of black writers from the States that included James Baldwin and Richard Wright. Himes's autobiography, *The Quality of Hurt,* written after he'd moved to Spain, was published the same year as *White Man's Justice, Black Man's Grief.*

Donnie's Chester character bore no striking resemblance to Himes, aside from his name and the fact that he had served time. Chester Hines had no creative talents whatsoever. Donnie made him into a professional killer and stickup man who would have cashed in on a liquor store robbery had he not been arrested that week. Chester shows little regret for having killed his fat ex-wife— during their honeymoon, no less—by forcing her overboard the boat from which he fished. Only vivid nightmares involving his violent trip north as a young man and other episodes from his past seem to disturb Chester. The dreams appear as a sort of metaphor for the control the character lacks, as it pertains to his ultimate fate as a habitual offender in a court system that functions by double standard. For all of Chester's contact with the system and all of the insightful predictions he makes, he is as helpless as any other convict by the book's final page. Donnie's reflections of the joint while writing *White Man's Justice, Black Man's Grief* revealed his intimate familiarity with incarceration. For what the actual story lacked, the details composed an intriguing portrait from the other side of the concrete wall. It would have been nearly impossible for anyone besides Donnie to know how many of the inmate characters, who included rapists and homosexuals, had been creations of his mind. To be certain, there were jailed men whose circumstances resembled those of every character in the book. A few had even committed the same types of violations for which Donnie was sent to the joint. There was a fine line for him to walk in creating stories that were credibly realistic yet still obscured truths that it was best to avoid making more publicly known.

Black Girl Lost came in January 1974. The novel, which depicted a life of neglect that virtually forces a pretty teenager to seek survival by doing crime, revealed a level of compassion for the adolescent that he hadn't shown in any of his five previous books. Despite her scheming and lawlessness, she easily became the most sympathetic character Donnie had been able to craft. In the meantime, bill collectors showed Donnie and Shirley little sympathy. It was more than a notion to maintain their family's apartment unit in the house on Cortland. At one point, things got so tight that Shirley made the decision to help bring in some additional cash. She went back out on the streets. It wouldn't have been Donnie's first choice to have his woman spreading her legs for money the same way his whores had done, but he accepted it. Prostitution became a temporary solution to their problems. At least Shirley was still coming home to her man.

With the arrival of the New Year came a new sense of encouragement in the city of Detroit. Coleman Alexander Young—the political firebrand who had once made the House Committee reps attempting to label him a Communist practically curse God for creating black men—took office as the first black mayor on January 1. The white residents who remained in the city were largely disapproving. With his foul tongue and often brash manner, Young would fit everything but the traditional image of a mayor. Black Detroit, nonetheless, saw him as a liberator who would give them a sense of ownership in the city. Far beyond the municipal boundaries, there were economic ramifications that had a ripple effect. Detroit held down about 20 percent of the nation's automotive employment, but the oil crisis that would take place that year negatively affected the manufacturing of vehicles. There were about 1.6 million industry jobs in the metro area, many held by young, black men and women. Among them were workers who had gone to the plants directly from high school. Assembly lines represented stability for many a household and many a family member, who stayed clothed and fed. But the nationwide economic recession threatened general welfare. Seemingly oblivious, Donnie continued to crank out books at a staggering pace. He was a virtual assembly line of paperbacks. *Crime Partners, Death List,* and *Eldorado Red* were released just weeks apart. *Eldorado Red* told the story of a big-time numbers operator. Red employs his own staff of money handlers, bet takers and enforcers, who sustain themselves almost entirely through his illegal gambling resources. When the boss is betrayed by his own son, he demands a form of restitution that ends in murder. Unlike the protagonists in most of Donnie's stories, however, Red is not given any comeuppance in the end. Problems are corrected to his satisfaction, and he suffers no consequence for his complicity in the retaliation.

In his own life, Donnie felt less secure about recriminatory measures. It was becoming tough to narrate fiction without exposing actual crimes and criminals he had encountered through the years. There were hustlers who still operated on the same streets as when they'd first stepped outside the law. His books could be regarded as a form of snitching if Donnie didn't check himself sufficiently. Again, he scrawled his thoughts about a book that, upon further reflection, he may or may not have chosen to complete. Again, as he had done at the start of his career, he sought help from a sister. The undated writing read: "Hard to stay away from truth! Could get hurt. Know to[o] much. Be careful in the life. If they read this, can tell who story is about—middle of story. Called Marie for advi[c]e. Change storyline—no brothers, one person—change city and drug used. May not finish this one." With the proliferation of pushers and dope houses, many of which he had visited, it was possible that he had begun using some of his own connections as models of study. He could feel the danger creeping into his life. It was a perception that would increase as the year gradually expired.

On May 11, 1974, Donnie called Joanie into the house. He approached his younger sister with an assignment that he felt was too important to handle by himself. Joanie was expecting that Donnie wanted to start a new book. Instead, on that day when he pulled her aside, he asked her for help in writing his last will and testament. It was an assignment she would never forget. She was daunted by the notion of having the only other male figure who was biologically closest to her taken away.

"What's wrong, Donnie?" she asked, taking him seriously. "Are you sick?"

"Tomorrow is not promised to anyone, Poopty. You never know when your time is up."

Despite the long-time presence of his demon, his vice in the form of a needle, Donnie had always appeared to be in relatively good physical health. He never showed any outward sign of addiction, at least nothing that was detectable by the average observer. Of course, excluding his cautionary demonstrations to Joan and young Charles. Now, though, Joan thought her brother was deteriorating before her eyes. With his habit, at times, creeping up to hundreds of dollars a day, he lost weight. Long gone were the out-of-sight suits, shoes, and other fine threads he had worn as if they were uniforms when he had made his living illegally. Donnie was a different man. He had operated on the fringe, and the center was unfamiliar territory. Walking on the edge gave him a peculiar sense of grounding that more structured settings never could. A

psychologist might have been able to explain it, where none of the
people who'd known him most of his life were up to the task. Donnie had always preferred to create his own agenda. With whatever
he gained in the secure legitimacy he found as a writer, the profession still lacked that freedom to work exactly when, where, and in
what manner he pleased. He wrote to survive, and combined with
his daily struggles and responsibilities, survival had become pretty
overwhelming. Having hit the charts with lighter material, Marvin
Gaye sang of the condition that described Donnie's emotional
state, probably better than a well-qualified shrink ever could have
with his 1971 recording "Inner City Blues."

> *Hang-ups*
> *Letdowns*
> *Bad breaks*
> *Setbacks . . .*
> *Yeah, make me wanna holler, the way they do my life*
> *This ain't livin' . . .*
> *No, no, baby, this ain't livin'*

For Donnie, this wasn't living. He knew he was mainly responsible for the depressing state in which he found himself. It was not
by coincidence that one of his final creations, a character named
Johnny Washington, faced the challenge of finding a way to support his survival and that of his family. In resemblance to Gaye's
song, Donnie would title the last book *Inner City Hoodlum,* and
would use, as always, his personal experiences to map out the character's path. It was ironic and hurtful that he controlled the lives of
one-dimensional men and women but felt so helpless to control his
own. The written will would be Donnie's most important piece of
nonfiction. Joanie settled down at the typewriter to begin the unpleasant job. As they collaborated on the document, she and Donnie began to talk. And they laughed. The levity arose as if from out
of nowhere. Perhaps it was meant as a blessing of time together
between siblings, because, in the end, the pledges on paper would

be all Donnie could leave behind. Across the top of the first page, Joanie typed "MY WILL & Testament." It began with the words, "To Whom it may concern."

> *If I should die, I would like for this to be my will, since I haven't had one made. Each novel of mine will be left to someone I consider close to me, and since I am of sound [mind], I pray that this letter is followed just as I dictate it here. First—Dopefiend. The royalty money off of Dopefiend should be put in an account for Donna Sailor, my daughter, until she reaches the age of eighteen, then she can use it for college or whatever else she might choose. Second— Whoreson. . . . This novel goes to my son Alfonso Chambers, or Alfonso Goines, whichever. He should receive the [royalty] money off of this book whenever he turns eighteen, and continue to receive it until the book leaves the market. Third—Black Gangster. . . . The money from this book should be put up in a fund for Christopher Howard, my son, until he is eighteen, then he can use the money any way he chooses. [Fourth]—Street Player[s]. . . . Donnie, or Donald, Howard, my son. The rights of this novel should be put in a fund until he reaches the age of eighteen; then it becomes his. Fifth— White Man's Justice, Black [M]an's [G]rief. This novel, or money from it, goes to Tony Howard, into a fund until he becomes eighteen.*

In the will, Donnie also revealed his connection to another child, the last he would so publicly name. His lecherous ways with women had left him frequently open to the chance of paternity, and the family began to privately wonder about even some of those he claimed. But knowing Donnie, it may have been hard even for *him* to keep track of the ladies with whom he'd been involved, so if the mothers became distant, there was no way for Joe and Myrtle to be sure they weren't missing out on a grandchild. Or for Marie and Joan to know how they might contact a niece or a nephew. At the least, Donnie could be given credit for trying to be responsible. In death—in the form of regular financial payments from Holloway House—perhaps he could be a more stable and dependable provider than he had been in life.

Nine—Eldorado Red—Tabatha Peterson, or Sanders, my daughter by Sandra Peterson, I want her to receive the royalty money from Eldorado Red. The money should be put in a fund until she reaches eighteen, then she may use it as she sees fit.

Through whatever the circumstances, Donnie's parents and sisters would hear almost nothing from the girl or her mother in the years to come. And possibly the last thing on Donnie's burdened mind was chasing down the pair. He did well to hold together as much of the household he and Shirley maintained. Besides, he had never been one for overextending himself where family and children were concerned. He wasn't keen on big holiday gatherings and the like. He was not the relative who was generally expected to show up at Christmas dinner with an armful of gifts. Donnie's generosity had been frequently overshadowed by various other preoccupations. He willed the royalties from *Black Girl Lost* to Shirley, while *Crime Partners* and *Death List* were assigned to Myrtle. Donnie also included Marie's daughter, Jean, and Joan's boys, Michael and Patrick. Among the last named to beneficiary status in the will was an old companion. He hadn't pimped, begged for baked goods, and shared apartments with Donnie the way Walter had, yet he had been one of those who Donnie found reliable when needed:

Eleven—Never [D]ie [A]lone. . . . Because of his friendship over the years, I leave the royalties from this novel, Never Die Alone, to Albert Clark, known as Crummie. My personal friend.

A few close observers had actually questioned the level and nature of Clark's devotion to Donnie. The author had given him perhaps the highest manner of tribute by placing his name on the covers of four books, *Crime Partners*, *Death List*, *Cry Revenge*, and *Kenyatta's Escape*. He completed novels so rapidly that Holloway House became concerned about the possibility of his books flooding the market. Teenagers and adults were increasingly drawn to his work, which—on one of its deepest levels—reflected much about the times in which they were living and the manner in which everyday, poor, struggling people functioned. Donnie had developed a following that would continue to grow, but his publishers wanted to do their best to keep his products from competing with one another. Bentley Morriss made a suggestion.

"Donald, God love you," he said. "We want to publish the books, but if you put out too many books of an author within a given period of time it has a sham about it. Would you consider putting a book out under a pseudonym?"

Donnie thought about it. Crummy's name should be as good as any. Holloway House first published the titles as if they were written by Al C. Clark. Then they began to put out the attribution of Al C. Clark "as told to Donald Goines." That the books would sell was the greatest concern of all parties involved. It didn't matter in the slightest that Crummy would never write a book for Holloway House as long as he lived. For his sons, Donnie added a stipulation to the will that would ensure his family name continued after he was gone. On its final page, he specified:

If, by chance, I complete any other novels before my death, I wish the royalties from them to go to my oldest son, Alfonso Chambers. If, by chance, anything should happen to anyone that I have left novels [to], the [rights] of these books are not to be passed on by them. The rights to my novels should come back to Marie, Myrtle, Alfonso Goines family. Before any of my children shall receive any money from [my] novels, their last name should be legally changed so that they will be Goines. If they do not [choose] to [accept] this name, then the money should remain in a fund to be shared among the other Goines. Each and every one of my sons shall have his name changed to Goines before receiving his share of [benefits]. The only way that they don't have their names changed will be because they couldn't have it done legally. That will be the only excuse, that for some reason the courts wouldn't allow them to change their names. As far as the girls are concerned, it's not really necessary, but for Alfonso, Tony, Donnie, Chris, these boys should try and have their names changed to Goines.

With its last word typed, Joan was the first to sign the writer's final requests as a witness. At the time, she had no way to recognize how important her help in completing the task had been. Her brother's literary legacy would ultimately become a source of both pride and pain within the family. Perhaps revealing the sensitivity he felt toward his siblings, Donnie wrote *Swamp Man.* It was the only novel that he would set outside of the urban environments with which he was so familiar. Instead, the story develops against the backdrop of a small, rural Mississippi community. In one chapter, Donnie described the moment when *Swamp Man's* main character recognizes that his sister has been drugged:

> *The Henrietta he knew wouldn't have let him see her in her bra, let alone stark naked. The more he thought of it, the angrier he became. The sight of Henrietta dancing naked, stripped of her pride and womanhood, fed fuel to his anger . . . Now he realized why they had been able to take advantage of her.*

Donnie hadn't always approved of his sisters' choices. Whatever protective instincts Donnie may have developed were probably well formed, if not well directed. He had contributed his share of negative influence to the lives of any number of women, and more than likely he had come across some who called themselves someone's sisters. He knew what a man with game was capable of running because he had run it. In the Henrietta character, he represented the vulnerability he perceived as a common attribute of women in general. In more than a dozen novels, he had depicted only one female as a protagonist, in *Black Girl Lost,* and as the title implied, she was one of dubious strength and distinction from the others. George Jackson, *Swamp Man's* lead, is driven to take bloody vengeance on the men who gang-rape Henrietta, in a violent, perverse, and gripping yet difficult-to-read tableau that stretches over several pages.

> *"By God, Zeke, look at them tits on her, will you?" Jamie stated, taking one of them in his hand and squeezing it until she cried out.*

"I ain't seen none like that in some time, I'll tell yo', boy. Them crit-ters stand right on up there!"

"Damn them tits," Zeke cried out, spit running out of the corners of his mouth and dropping down on the half-naked woman. He reached around him and ran his hand down the front of her pants, playing in the tightly curled hairs he found there.

Finally, she could feel herself being dragged down to the ground. Rough hands tore her pants off her body until she lay naked under the branches of the tall willow tree. Birds flew overhead calling out to each other, but Henrietta heard nothing as she felt fingers being rammed up inside her body. She called out, screamed for mercy, begged and promised, but to no avail. The men didn't hear. Her panic meant nothing to them. They were beyond stopping. Their only desire now was lust.

Similarly, a few books later, Donnie showed his awareness of the bond between father and daughter as he set *Daddy Cool's* primary character, Larry Jackson, on the warpath after the man he holds responsible for turning his daughter out onto the street. With what paternal sensibilities Donnie possessed, he portrayed Larry as the prototypical image of the concerned and protective father:

Many times, Daddy Cool had sat in his poolroom and listened to this same young man talk about his exploits with the young girls of the neighborhood. Now the young man was spending his time with Janet. He had warned the girl about the boy, but she hadn't paid any attention to him, thinking he was being old-fashioned. She loved the attention she received when she and the self-proclaimed pimp rode through the neighborhood with the top down.

Whether Donnie did it consciously or without thought, he gave several different characters in his books identical names. For example, Larry's right hand was called Earl, just like the hustler in *Street Players*. There was more than one Willie Brown. More than one Janet, Red, Buddy, and Mike. Even more than one man called "Preacher." Another characteristic of Donnie's prose was the awkward placement of physical descriptions. As if it were the one instruction his editors had driven into his mind, he routinely assigned attributes like "tall, light-complexioned" or "short, muscular" to the images he put on paper. But he frequently added the phrases to sentences that were irrelevant to outward appearance. His work was often edited with a fairly heavy hand; however, the editing itself was not of a particularly high quality, as misspellings and errors in grammar and punctuation made the final prints. Readers, nonetheless, generally responded with eager acceptance. The raw and simplistic language Donnie used complemented the subject matter of his novels, adding a perceived authenticity to the fiction. He briefly wrote to himself: "When I'm mellow, stories come and go—so many, like I'm seeing a movie." There were folks who regarded themselves as Donald Goines fans. Who went out to pick up the next book as quickly as they could finish one. Holloway House would receive letters from readers expressing their admiration, and there came a point when Donnie was even regarded as a neighborhood celebrity of sorts. What he lacked in wealth, he was gradually gaining in status.

Ironically, this is when it got more painful for him. The buzz about his books and ongoing success with getting published interfered with Donnie's anonymity. At one time, he had been able to go out and score from a dealer, return home, and work until he grew tired, without any thought of the buy he made earlier. Now, though, there were pushers who recognized his name and face, not because he was a regular, but because of the little notoriety he was achieving. Donnie's pride was wounded in ways it had never previously been. Young niggers were moving into the heroin game, and if a level of arrogance was detected in them, it could be tough for an old player to handle. When Donnie found himself compelled to patronize the neighborhood boys, he carried the added shame of knowing that they could brag and talk shit about how he needed them as suppliers. As he asked for money to make the buy, he would face Walter in tears, grown-man tears that begged an answer to the question of how he had reached such a miserably low point. Walter would give him what cash he could and try to encourage his old friend. A junkie had it hard as hell when he knew his sickness was out of reach yet felt powerless to contain it. Donnie had pronounced his own fate a few years earlier in the first chapter of *Dopefiend*. Now he felt it approaching him. As he had done demonstratively within his own family, he offered the equivalent of a testimonial for all of his readers to heed. The most definitive public statement he would ever make about the source of his own addiction:

> *The white powder looked innocent as it lay there in the open, but this was the drug of the damned, the curse of mankind. Heroin, what some call "smack," others "junk," "snow," "stuff," "poison," "horse." It had different names, but it still had the same effect. To all of its users, it was slow death.*

By contrast, the Kenyatta series symbolized Donnie's desire for victory. It revealed a sense of morality that he seldom displayed in his actions. Young and militant, Kenyatta was first introduced in *Crime Partners*. While his approach resembles that of gangsters and terrorists, he is named after Jomo Kenyatta, leader of the movement that brought the African nation of Kenya to freedom from British colonialists in the 1950s. In one chapter of *Crime Partners*, Kenyatta, operating as a gun supplier, tells two would-be customers: "You brothers are dedicated, but not to gettin' rid of these white pigs that ride around our neighborhood acting like white gods." He promises the men that if they participate in a vigilante mission he has planned for that evening, he will give them the weapons they want. Intrigued by the leader, who models his organization much like the Black Panther Party, the characters accept his offer. Kenyatta is devoted not only to eliminating police brutality but also to ridding his community of drugs. As a matter of fact, *Death List* finds him in an alliance with the cops in an effort to ice various dealers. A desire for freedom from all epidemics and vice is what drives him. Like Kenyatta, Donnie longed for liberation. The character represented the strength and fearless determination that he lacked.

Donnie maintained few pastimes, but he remained a competitive chess player. Walter regularly stopped by his place to challenge him to a game or two. At times, the men would make wagers as if they were playing cards. Not a man who had objections to gambling, Donnie put up what he could to keep the stakes respectable, if not high. Here, he would show flashes of his old self, which was not altogether a bad thing. If there were opportunities when he could show himself and others that he was still sharp, that he still had the hustler's edge, his confidence might increase to a degree that would let him believe he could pull the other suffering areas of his life together. Donnie and Walter might face off at opposite ends of the chess board with a lure of twenty dollars per game. During one of their meetings, Walter couldn't help but notice how much his opponent appeared to be in need of a fix. Donnie sat with two of the children on his lap while they played. He scratched frantically at his arm, obviously distracted. Walter was getting the best of him in the game. Donnie continued to scratch. Shirley noticed and suggested that he go into the bathroom to take care of his jones. Donnie didn't move far from the table, but finally he gave in to the urge. As Walter turned his head in disgust, Donnie tied off his arm, located a vein and began the bloody process of injection. He laughed at Walter's squeamishness. Then, relieved, he turned his attention to the board and kicked Walter's ass.

Their game suffered greater interruption on a different occasion. While the men carefully worked their strategies against one another, they gave no thought to who was approaching the house outside. The unit that Donnie and Shirley occupied was a lower that could be entered only by way of the alley. Their building was not especially conspicuous among others in the neighborhood. If bad intentions could be visibly identified, however, three visitors who sought Donnie as they walked up to the house should have attracted notice. The men were let into the house, and Donnie recognized them right away. He abruptly excused himself from the chess competition and led the men into the bathroom, where he closed the door for privacy. Still, Walter could hear parts of the conversation. There had been an unsettling tension in the air since the tall, menacing, hillbillylike figures first appeared.

"I know I did you wrong," Walter could hear Donnie saying.

"My family's here. Give me a few days." Clearly, Donnie was attempting to negotiate his way out of a situation. There was no telling what kind of dilemma he might have created for himself. But Walter felt it was a serious one. Donnie emerged from the bathroom, and his visitors left in peace. However, they had found him—and for whatever the reason they came—it hadn't been to take any decisive action. Donnie had bought himself some time. With Walter's mind engaged over what he had witnessed, his partner briefly broke the situation down: Donnie's three visitors had come from California to find him. He had crossed someone before he left the state, and the transgression was obviously not appreciated. Donnie didn't offer many more details, but it was a discussion Walter wouldn't forget. When he left the house, in spite of the disturbing and peculiar episode, he had no way of knowing that he and Donnie had played their final game together.

In the weeks that followed, Donnie stayed in the grind. His writing career had become a vastly different reality than the one he envisioned five years earlier when his every movement was still under the supervision of the state. The moderate success of his work notwithstanding, Donnie had not achieved a measure of wealth or fame that would be sufficient to alter his lifestyle the way he hoped it would. Apart from his meeting with Marie Teasley, he had received virtually zero media exposure. There was the one interview broadcast on a community radio station, but nothing that had given him household-name status. In *Never Die Alone*, Donnie introduced Paul Pawlowski, his only Caucasian protagonist. The character had a contrived and peculiar name to go along with bright, blue eyes and the face of a "Jewish Polack bastard." Certainly, he bore no outward resemblance to Donnie. Yet, while most of his other creations on paper were inspired by the criminal persona he had once worn, Paul was a thinly veiled reflection of who Donnie had become.

. . . he remembered that he was going on an interview for a job, and that he might not have to wait for his next royalty check from his publishers for his two paperback books . . . Sometimes he had a few extra dollars in March or September when his royalty checks

*arrived. But the other months were hell, unless the writer happened
to be a good money manager. But to find a writer who could manage
money was rare, because anyone who was adept at it would also
have enough common sense to pick a better livelihood.*

A struggling freelance journalist, Paul lives in New York City. His
relatively mundane existence in a seedy neighborhood and shitty,
little apartment—where a coffeepot serves as his sole companion—
is about to change. A fascinating encounter takes place as the plot
of *Never Die Alone* rather slowly develops: Donnie represents his
own attempt at transformation in the chance meeting between
decent, well-meaning Paul and a cold-hearted, scamming hustler
called King David. Though it wasn't his occupation in the book,
King David was a well-known Detroit pimp with whom Donnie
had likely been familiar. He might not have intended it, but the
symbolism in the story is conspicuous. It was essentially a book in
which aspects of his inner self strangely clashed with one another.
Donnie seemed to be making a deliberate attempt to write a novel
that might broaden his appeal among fiction readers by cleverly
couching the hallmark drug and criminal elements within the con-
text of Paul's moral dilemmas and decision making. Meanwhile,
he—consciously or unconsciously—drew religious parallels in the
form of interaction between the book's two primary characters.
The story makes it difficult to miss the irony of a Jewish man meeting up with a slick cat called King David. Not unlike the great biblical ruler of Israel, throughout the story, King David's last name is
never used. Ultimately, Paul finds himself chosen by the conniving
hustler to carry out his last requests as he nears death. King David
leaves behind a journal in which he appears to have recorded the
disgusting transgressions and perverse acts he has committed
against others while in Los Angeles. Paul grows to detest the man
he gets to know through these writings, but in the end King David
offers redemption, much like the biblical David offered his people.
Paul finds a way to use the hustler's legacy in a way that will benefit
folks resembling those whose lives the dealer helped ruin. The story
was further testimony of the personal victory Donnie desired for

himself. Its conclusion was also an indictment against the drug dealers, who made it all the more difficult for addicts like him to be free. These pushers supplied junkies with dope that was designed to keep them hooked and coming back for more.

Donnie probably never considered it, but his addictive personality may well have been genetic. It wouldn't have been a horrible stretch to categorize his father's work ethic as habitual. Joe handled his cleaning and pressing duties until his health began to fail. The old man was hospitalized and treated with what means and provisions the medical staff could make available to him. Yet, with their patient having neared his ninth decade on Earth, the strength and condition of his body was not such that a recovery and return to the cleaning store was in the realm of likelihood. Big Joe died at eighty-eight. Family members were at his bedside. Donnie wept uncontrollably, the tears washing over his face. In spite of all the years of emotional distance between them, he loved his father. And now that Joe was gone, there would be no chance of rebuilding a relationship, no chance for Donnie to feel that he had truly made his father proud of the man he became. He hurt over the loss, probably in ways that were very different from the grief that Joe's other children felt. In at least some respects, their father had been the most dominant presence in any of their lives. Donnie was the only boy born to him and Myrtle, and if he had regrets, there was no chance of his letting them both see how he hoped to finally represent them as a son. Donnie felt the force of grief again at Joe's funeral. Charles and his band were somewhere performing at the time, so he didn't return to Detroit to pay his last respects. Before the end of that sad October month, he would miss a second burial held for another loved one. This time, it would not be the funeral of an old man.

Premonition was the sort of thing that came now and then in the Goines family. They couldn't always know when it would appear or how to prepare once it did. In Donnie's case, there was no apparent redeeming value in getting such signs. He received at least one on the day of his father's last rites. Perhaps it had become lost in a cloud of thought and anxiety. The stress Donnie felt was apparent when he handwrote: "Buried Daddy today. Mama back in hospital. Trying to get right. Take care Mama, Wea Wea, and Joan, my children and Shirley. Need more money. Asked publisher to send me away anywhere so I can do better. Wong has gotten stronger. Joan made me a lemon pie. I can stay upstairs and write more. I have to work fast. Almost pawned typewriter today. I feel like something is going to happen. Did not pawn it. Mama is doing OK. Marie went home. Told her husband and Bobby I'm next." The thoughts were, typically, rather disjointed, yet the sense of some urgency was there.

Such statements as "I have to work fast" and "I feel like something is going to happen" were not the kinds of things he had typed or scribbled onto the nearest sheet of paper in the past. Moreover, the concern about creating security for his loved ones stemmed from more than Joe's death. To be sure, his father had been a symbol of stability in the family, but now Donnie was thinking seriously about the future. It was, in a way, remarkable that a deteriorating junkie could even consider taking responsibility for others, but what kind of a legacy for his loved ones might he leave behind? And how could he make certain it was anything that would be worth leaving? Myrtle had developed heart problems that together with her diabetes further jeopardized her health. Joe had worked until the years that had piled up on his body created a drain too tough for any man of nearly ninety, let alone one who became ill, to withstand. Myrtle wouldn't be able to handle the dry cleaners on her own. The family business her husband had carried for so long, the one he had hoped his offspring would continue to operate, would be permanently closed. "To do better," as Donnie wrote, had been on his mind for at least a year. If he could do better, he could handle a lot more obligation: his own and at least part of the family's. What loomed most ominous was the statement his older sister was said to have made after returning to Dayton, Ohio, where she and Warren had moved. Donnie wasn't prepared to die, and if he was indeed "next" to be buried, he would have to get himself together in a hurry.

If he told himself the truth, on October 18 change was starting to happen. "Sent unfinished story to Marie," he wrote. "Ask[ed] her to read and keep it. Joan is fine. I'm winning my fight with wong. Played chess—I won." Of course, Donnie had felt his strength rising before but had fallen short when he tried to kick on his own. There could be no way of knowing with certainty whether this time would be any different from the others. At least one person, however, knew that Donnie had gone out to score around the time that he claimed to be gaining ground against his addiction. One night, Ralph, who was a brother-in-law to Shirley, accompanied Donnie on a run to buy a fix. They rode to a house in one section of the Trumbull Avenue and Forest area. Trumbull was an older thoroughfare that stretched from near downtown westward. Ralph didn't know much about the particular address or this particular dealer. He knew of Donnie's habit and, in fact, thought nothing of the brief stop. But he would recall it with disturbing clarity only weeks later. There was nothing particularly unusual about the Monday night, three days after he made his random, penciled documentation. All was relatively calm at 232 Cortland inside the Goines and Sailor apartment, at least by outward appearance. Shirley prepared dinner. She called Joan to ask for advice about cooking some greens, but Joan was preoccupied and told Shirley she would call her back later. The women had gotten along pretty well. Shirley decided on a basic beef-and-potato meal. Donnie and the children were all there with her when, sometime after dinner, probably two or more gunmen entered the building. Most likely, from the time the shooters arrived, no one inside had much of a chance to breathe long. The attack had what many later believed to be the appearance of a hit.

That occasional Goines premonition was sparked again on the morning of October 22. This time, it was abruptly manifest in Joanie's otherwise tranquil thoughts. David had answered the phone while she was in the bathroom. He went to the door to speak to her. He had horrible news, he informed her. Joan looked at her husband.

"Donnie's dead," she said quietly.

David somehow acknowledged.

"And Shirley, too," Joan added, only half asking. She had forgotten to call Shirley back about the greens, not knowing it would be the last time they spoke. Donnie and Shirley had both been shot repeatedly. Highland Park cops said an anonymous caller reported their deaths. Out of mercy, haste in leaving the scene, or perhaps because they had been hidden, the murderers left the two children who were in the house unharmed. They were found locked in the basement. Detectives who were sent to 232 Cortland identified no immediate suspects or motives. Still, the authorities needed a family member to come to the crime scene. In all her years of nursing-care experience, Joanie hadn't become comfortable with death. Marie would have to return to Detroit, as she had just weeks earlier when they buried her daddy. Walter and Ralph got word. They went to the house, along with Shirley's family. The mix of friends, relatives, police, and medical officials created a stirring appearance. Sounds of grief could be heard inside the apartment. Cops made an effort to control the comings and goings of those gathered at the four-family address. If there had been any occupants in the other units at the time the shots were fired, they apparently had done nothing to intervene. No one came forward. The days and weeks that followed the murders would be hurtful ones for those who loved the two victims, but not days and weeks filled with any leads or information that would result in arrests.

The following morning's *Detroit News* made little of the killings, grouping Donnie's and Shirley's deaths with a third, unrelated homicide for the headline "3 murdered in Highland Park." Briefly written, the article made no mention of Donnie's books or his popularity as a writer, citing only that his age was "unknown." Most likely, the reporter and others in the newsroom had never heard of him. The article mentioned that the killing was believed to be drug-related and that officers removed unspecified drug paraphernalia from the house. Such details were not revealing to anyone who knew Donnie. No news report could have really told the story that was most significant anyway: what he might have been were it not for his drug addiction; what he had strived to become, in spite of it. As the word of Donnie's demise got around, there was a good deal of sadness in the community among the folks who had enjoyed his work, collected each novel. Yet, to the unfamiliar, in the media and elsewhere, his death was short of tragic. To be sure, many of them regarded him as just another dead junkie. His people, on the other hand, would always know him as more. Marie was listed as the informant on the death certificate, which described the manner of her brother's passing, along with a brief sketch of the man who was killed. It requested his address, parents' names, things like that. One section of the death certificate asked for a listing of the deceased person's occupation. In the rectangular space, a clerk typed "Writer." It was the single word that had driven Donnie to find his way back from the missteps he had taken during the previous twenty years.

Legacy: An Epilogue

*Ecrire seize romans durant les quatre dernieres annees de sa vie ne
l'a pas empeche' de faire fructifier ses affaires courantes . . .*

*[Writing sixteen novels during the last four years of his life did
not prevent him from pursuing his usual preoccupations . . .]*

*Sil n'existait qu'une couleur, peutetre serait-ce; le noir de l'ennui,
du desespoir, de la nuit et de la couleur de la peau.*

*[If there existed only one color, perhaps it would be black; the
black of boredom, of desperation, of the night and of the color of
the skin.]*

—French excerpts of Donald Goines's book reviews

I don't like cemeteries. Never have. Aphorisms like the one suggesting that the graveyard is the safest place a person can go are
not comforting. Superstitions—that burial-ground dirt should
never be carried from the site, for example—don't move me, either. In the first place, fear has really never been what causes my
aversion. I've got good enough sense to know that cemetery residents are nothing but dead people. That's probably why I have always felt like my presence there was inappropriate. Like a violation
of some sacred privacy. It's a voyeuristic feeling, especially when,
out of curiosity, I find myself reading the names on headstones of
people I never knew. From there, I often let my eyes wander to the
dates of birth and death in a nearly unconscious attempt to calcu-
late how long or short their lives were. After that I might imagine
all sorts of things about the individual, which wouldn't likely
have been my business when they were above ground, let alone

now. But the thoughts linger as I distract myself, trying not to step on anybody's loved one, as I walk to the plot where my family or friends are gathered for whatever burial has brought me there.

On this sunny February afternoon, though, it's a different story. I've been planning to make this visit to Detroit Memorial Cemetery for about two years. As a matter of fact, I am going there specifically for the purpose of looking at headstones and grave markers. Quite a few of my own people are there. Two sets of great-grandparents. My uncle Robert. Ben Crain, the grandfather who spoiled me until I was ten, and Toy Collier Allen, the grandmother who died before I was born. This is also where one of my literary ancestors was laid to rest. Donald Joseph Goines is buried at Detroit Memorial, but his family doesn't recall exactly where. As a military veteran, he was supposed to be given a headstone to go along with his survivor's benefits; I'm told it was never issued. His marker might be covered with overgrown grass and weeds. This unknown place beneath the soil strikes me as a metaphor for Mr. Goines's life. He kept the people who loved him guessing where he might wind up. I feel ready for the challenge of looking for him, nevertheless. His sisters don't know it, but I had intended to ask them if they'd ride to the cemetery with me. Marie Richardson informed me, however, that they had made a trip there several months earlier. A group of independent filmmakers came to the city to interview her and Joan Coney and to record a short documentary. They showed me a videotape of the piece after we'd all gotten together for dinner one Saturday evening. There is no Detroit Memorial footage in the piece they showed me. They had looked for Mr. Goines's marker with no success.

If not for my research, I wouldn't be any more interested in this visit than in other similar ones I've made, particularly since I'm not certain that I'll find what I'm after. It just wouldn't feel right to me if I didn't make an effort to be in some part of Mr. Goines's presence, having come to know him in the unusual way that I have through papers and memories.

Then, it occurs to me that I may have a problem if I go to Detroit Memorial unannounced and ask questions about the whereabouts of a person who is not my blood relative. I've never done this sort of thing before, and maybe it won't be as simple as just showing up and getting assistance. Presumably, there's a record of the men, women, and children interred there, but how public this record is, I have no idea. I can only imagine that the attendants would be people who have a good deal of patience and consideration, though it's possible that I'm wrong. I decide I'd better make a call before I go downstairs to my car.

The years following Mr. Goines's murder have been marked mostly by financial disputes, additional family tragedies, and significant success that, unfortunately, he can never personally enjoy. Two more books were published in 1975, the year after his death. One that became a personal favorite of mine was *Kenyatta's Last Hit*, in which Mr. Goines kills his alter ego. The book's conclusion is particularly sad for me, not so much because the character dies, but because it seems on some level to be the author's statement about the futility of fighting against oppressive forces in a nihilistic, capitalist society. In a manner similar to the way Mr. Goines left this world, he described Kenyatta's murder:

> *The guard in the corner of the room pulled the trigger of his .45. The bullet struck Kenyatta in the back of the head, sending pieces of his shattered skull flying against Clement's oak desk. With half his head shot away, Kenyatta tumbled forward and fell onto the superb shag rug.*

Posing as a drug dealer, Kenyatta travels from California to Las Vegas just so he can get close enough to Clement Jenkins, one of the biggest pushers on the West Coast, to put him on ice. The fact that Kenyatta meets his death disappointed me on two levels: first, because he was a metaphor for Mr. Goines's desire to overcome his addiction to drugs; second, because it suggests that good can never defeat the larger societal evils that afflict our black communities. Not even in fiction. The other book published in 1975 was *Inner*

City Hoodlum. Mr. Goines had been contracted to complete the novel for Holloway House at the time when he was killed. The unfinished manuscript and editing was completed by Carleton Hollander, who I'm told went on to work as a screenwriter in the Los Angeles area. He was brought into the Holloway House project under circumstances that would later be a point of contention with the Goines family. It was my understanding that Hollander took the Johnny Washington protagonist and others in the story to tie *Inner City Hoodlum*'s plot together. Mrs. Myrtle Goines became the administratrix for her son's estate, and she was sent a form with the heading of "Release and Consent to Use of Name." The document requested permission for the publisher to have "the irrevocable right, privilege and authority" to list Mr. Goines as the book's author, despite its identification of Hollander as "the writer of 'Inner City Hoodlum.'" In exchange for granting this right, the agreement provided 20 percent of the book's royalties to Mrs. Goines. Her name is signed to the document.

Myrtle Theresa Goines died in 1991. Not long passed before Marie Richardson took the opportunity to see if there was any way she could have the *Inner City Hoodlum* agreement nullified. A letter from a New York lawyer she contacted states: "In the confused set of facts, it seems that Holloway House is taking advantage of the name Donald Goines in exploiting books not written by him, and the monies that would otherwise be due to Mr. Goines's estate is being paid to the person they have hired to write under the name Donald Goines. . . . In my experience with book publishers, unless specifically agreed to by the original author, I know of no case where the original author's royalty, or any portion thereof, was paid to a writer who was retained by the publishing company to edit and/or re-write an author's works. It generally is paid out of the publisher's share of the monies received."

It was after Mrs. Goines's death that suspicions about the handling and disbursement of royalty revenue led to tension among Mr. Goines's survivors. Ms. Richardson spoke to me a lot about money, perhaps more than she realized. She told me she felt that, along with Holloway House, there were companies and newspapers all over the world that received profit from her brother's name, and she and her sister failed to benefit from this. No *legitimate* news publication, of course, would gain from the mere mention of any person, apart from the price of purchase by customers who picked it up. It became obvious to me, however, that Ms. Richardson saw the family's relationship to her brother as a matter of entitlement, as far as any profits were concerned. Perceived entitlement to money was the apparent cause of the distance that developed between Mr. Goines's siblings and his children.

They wound up seeking different probate lawyers after Mrs. Goines passed. She had been in charge of distributing the royalty payments to family members, in accordance with her son's will. With Mrs. Goines gone, room for conflict emerged. There were accusations that Mr. Goines's original will was altered. After almost ten years, I was told when I began my research, bad blood remained, literally and figuratively, between the relatives. Given different circumstances, it would have probably been simple enough to ask Ms. Richardson or her sister how to contact their nephews and nieces, but it was repeatedly explained to me that they had no communication with "the kids." Ms. Richardson said they hadn't done anything with their nieces and nephews, hadn't shared any good times with their brother's offspring since a family reunion in Little Rock during the early '90s. Ultimately, a court appointed co-trustee attorneys to represent the two sides of kin in a seven-year money quarrel. At one point, as much as $28,000 in royalties was withheld as the matter was sorted through. The closest I could get to any discussion of Mr. Goines's legacy by any of his sons or daughters was a quote from the November 2002 edition of a Chicago newspaper.

"I hear some people tell their kids they should not read this garbage," Donald Goines, Jr., reportedly told the weekly. "That's when I know they are misinterpreting. It's very educational for teenagers. Before they get started doing anything in the streets, they'll see what the consequences will be in the end." Regrettably, I wasn't able to locate him or any of his siblings to ask them for interviews. Not only was I late finding out that one daughter, Angela, who he had not named in the will, was listed in Mr. Goines's obituary as a survivor, I learned that at least one other of Mr. Goines's sons had become a habitual criminal, at one point serving in the same Jackson penitentiary that his father had, but he was reportedly attending school to get his life on course as of late 2002. Donna Sailor, the daughter of Mr. Goines and Shirley Sailor, was living in California, according to the last information any of my various sources could provide, but I could find no telephone listing or other record for her in the Los Angeles area. I noticed other Goines names in the metropolitan Detroit directory. When I tried to match them, however, the numbers were disconnected or assigned to new customers. I wanted to talk with them not only about any memories of their father, but also about who they felt might have been responsible for his death.

In the absence of eyewitnesses to the double killing, I sought feedback from other sources. As the weeks immediately following Mr. Goines's and Shirley Sailor's deaths passed, Mrs. Goines and her daughters heard rumors that two Polish brothers with whom the family had become acquainted from the neighborhood were behind the crimes. It was suspected that they went to 232 Cortland with plans to rob the author, thinking that he was accumulating wealth from book sales. But investigators never appeared to find such leads worth tracking. One of the men choked to death at the dinner table years later, Ms. Richardson was told. Apart from such theories, however, she and Ms. Coney remained in the dark about suspects. Out of a basic respect for the lives that were lost, and hoping to bring more details to the public light, I consulted an acquaintance for his qualified interpretation of the autopsy reports. Included with the findings were these investigative summaries, which placed Shirley Sailor in the kitchen and Mr. Goines in the living room:

> subject lying on kitchen floor face up, fully clothed—large smears of dried blood under body, dried blood on clothes—body cold & stiff—signs of struggle in home . . . Location is home of Shirley Sailor & Donald Goines, who apparently live together and have 2 children—Police received anonymous phone call that 2 people were

dead in this location—at time of police arrival—2 young siblings were in house with dead bodies—Police found identification of bodies in house—Police found large quantity of drug paraphernalia on premises—Police also recovered 1 shotgun, not believed to have been used in incident, although 1 spent shell casing was found outside of house. Also recovered were 2 38-cal revolvers from hallway floor—1 weapon had a capacity of 6 rounds—all of which were fired—2nd weapon had capacity of 5 rounds, of which three were live and 2 were fired.

Male subject has 5 wounds in body—2 in head, 1 in neck & 2 in chest—female subj. has 2 wounds in head—Police recovered 1 spent slug on floor in room . . . subject lying face up on floor in living room of home—fully clothed—body cold and stiff with large quantity of dried blood present on body and on floor under it—furniture in disarray—signs of a struggle

Contradicting the police report, the autopsy found that Shirley Sailor had been shot five times in the head and face. Craig Ciccone, a historian and student of political assassinations, told me this was one of the more significant findings. Ciccone lived in Highland Park, just blocks away from where the murders were committed. At the time we discussed the Goines and Sailor killings, Ciccone had devoted ten years to investigating the cowardly Chicago assassination of Black Panther Fred Hampton, who was shot to death by police while he slept in bed. Ciccone pointed out something about the medical examiner's findings related to Shirley Sailor that I had not considered: Her face and head were the only apparent targets of each wound she sustained.

"The grouping of the shots in her body is the greatest indication that this was a crime of passion," Ciccone said. "She was shot in the head, and they turned her over and shot her in the face. You'd have to be pretty stupid to shoot somebody in the face three times and not think they were already dead."

The description of her facial wounds suggests that Sailor was either lying flat or sitting with her head positioned flush against a surface, Ciccone explained. All of this raised a possibility that not one of the people I had interviewed about the murders ever suggested: that Shirley Sailor, not Donald Goines, was the primary target. There was nothing I ever read or heard that implied this to me, but without certainty of a motive, it had to be weighed. No information I received led me to believe that Ms. Sailor had even made any enemies, let alone enemies who might want to kill her. Nonetheless, Ciccone elaborated on his belief, which upon reflection I shared, that Sailor was murdered in a manner that emphasized the crime.

"The Mafia did that, too, especially for squealers," added Ciccone. Informers who were shot in the mouth, for example, were used to send a message to others who could potentially pose a problem in court. "It's an old sign that 'You're not gonna talk.'" Although Ms. Sailor was not shot in her mouth, the wounds to her face were inflicted at close range, in a fashion most commonly associated with retribution or the desired effect of horror.

"Either she was the target, or they were trying to send a message to Donald," Ciccone told me.

Mr. Goines was shot an identical number of times, but his face was unharmed. His body was displayed open-casket at Pope Funeral Home. A few of his novels were placed inside the burial casing. Holloway House later reproduced a gruesome-looking photo of his suited cadaver for next-edition covers of the first biography, *Donald Writes No More*. Most of the bullets that struck Mr. Goines went into his body, with one entering the head and another entering the neck. The presence of what are described as near-contact wounds, combined with the odd trajectory of the bullets in some places, suggests that Mr. Goines put forth a struggle. One chest wound in particular lends strength to the belief that he may have attempted, at one point, to rush the person pointing a pistol at him.

"Picture in your mind somebody charging a person with a gun," Ciccone said. "They're not going to aim for the head" to stop the target from charging. He said he believed Ms. Sailor was most likely killed first. It's harder to imagine that her wounds could have been placed in such close proximity to one another if she had seen or heard gunfire that was directed at Mr. Goines before she was attacked. Her physical movement to avoid the shots that struck her, or to put forth a struggle, would have likely created less precise and less directly placed points of entry for the bullets. Instead, only the soot detected on her right wrist, suggested that she raised her hand defensively. If, in the other possibility, Mr. Goines had been forced to watch his lady's execution or if he had heard the attack in the kitchen before a gunman could reach him in the living room, the appearance that he resisted and the difference in the wounds he sustained are more understandable. The "furniture in disarray," which the report mentions, almost certainly had to have been a result of Mr. Goines's movements, movements by the suspect or suspects, or a combination of both.

More absolute is the conclusion that no murder/suicide took place, Ciccone added. The fact that handguns were left at the scene might have been an attempt by the killers to leave the appearance that one or both of the victims were responsible for the deaths, or the weapons may have simply been dropped in haste. But I was also told that this was a characteristic of drug hits. Plausibly, no suicide victim could have the capacity to shoot himself or herself as many times and from as many angles as this couple was wounded. Besides, for all his frustrations and stress during the last year of his life, I never received the impression that Mr. Goines was suicidal or that he could be angered to the point of murdering his daughter's mother. This theory would find the least support of any that could be proposed as serious analysis of the crime. Still, there was an aspect of the report that Ciccone found peculiar. It was the description of both bodies as "cold and stiff," and the reference to dried blood. Neither the reports nor the medical examinations make mention of a specific time of death. Though the murders had to have occurred some time between the evening of October 21 and the morning of October 22, when it was reported, there is no estimation of an hour when the victims might have expired. Ciccone found it puzzling that there would have been time for the bodies to become cold and stiff or for the blood to dry without a report of the murders having been made sooner. While at least one person who went to the crime scene told me the children had been locked in the basement of the apartment, the report only indicates their presence in the unit, without indicating their location. Presumably, if they had discovered the dead bodies of their parents and guardians immediately, they would have contacted emergency officials by phone or gone to find other adult help long before rigor mortis could settle into both corpses.

My effort to gain information about the Goines and Sailor murders was the most challenging facet of all my research. Even though it's one of the first elements in writing the story that I began pursuing, after almost two years I found that my work had generated the least tangible of any results where the double homicide is concerned. My file folders are not nearly as thick with documents and data as I had once imagined they would be. In the corner of my desk, opposite the computer, I've got census papers, letters from the FBI, court records, prison papers, personal letters, and all sorts of other pieces to the puzzle that was Mr. Goines's life. Yet, I managed to get my hands on only a few pages of official documentation pertaining to the killings. Nonetheless, with all the difficulties Highland Park police have to handle, I can completely sympathize with the idea that any person calling around for information about a thirty-year-old, unsolved crime might be regarded as a nuisance. But I think I owe more to Mr. Goines and his family than to record everything I learned about his life, and then simply say that he was murdered.

I was thankful to be directed to Sergeant William McClain. He helped supervise a skeleton crew backed by the Wayne County Sheriff's Office and, later, by the Michigan State Police. If I began to irritate him with my questions, at least he didn't say so. Working from 6:00 P.M. to 6:00 A.M., Sergeant McClain had a little more time to spend talking with me on the phone than those on the day shift. But, like an idiot, I didn't realize until something like three months after I picked up the autopsy reports that the names of two detectives who were assigned to the homicides were included with the information I requested. Billy Quinn and Paul Lee were listed as the police investigators. I called Sergeant McClain one evening and reminded him of the last time he talked with me. "He *sounds* like a cop," I remember thinking. Like there couldn't be much he hadn't seen in his years of working metro Detroit. Cigarette smoke may have given his voice some of its husky gristle and distinction. McClain was one of few men still working who were on the force when the murders took place, though he didn't specifically recall it. In his way, patient and polite, he thought aloud about the last he had heard of Lee and Quinn. Lee was a mystery, he said. McClain had gotten no word from him nor received knowledge of his whereabouts in years and years. Quinn, on the other hand, was living in the Tampa area when he and the sergeant last had contact. A good while back, McClain had even visited with his former colleague in Florida, where they went fishing. He remembered that Quinn had gone into a sort of semiretirement, starting a glass-installation business that he operated while enjoying the sunshine far away from Michigan winters. But now I'd have to find him.

The whole thing was beginning to feel like a John Grisham novel, as if I'd become a character in one of those story lines about some determined amateur sleuth who has to rely on the kindness and cooperation of others he meets, in order to get information. Even if I could locate Billy Quinn, there was the matter of what he'd have to say, or whether he'd be willing to speak with me at all. And how much would he remember? As a news reporter, I had probably spent a little more time around police officers than the average person, but I just couldn't speculate on it. Weeks later, I checked my computer's e-mail and read a telephone number. A professional contact, who had already contributed generously to my research, called in a favor to someone who ran a check of Tampa and its surrounding areas. The search revealed more than fifty William Quinns, but only one Billy. Along with the name, he shared with me a birth date not quite two years after that of Mr. Goines. "I would think that might be about right, as 30 yrs ago he would be around 34 or so—about the age of an active-duty detective, I would think," my helpful acquaintance wrote. Soon, I would know if this was our man.

In a few days, I called and reached Quinn's wife. She screened me, explaining that she and her husband hadn't been in Detroit for twenty-five years. I told her why I was calling, and she confirmed that Quinn had been a Highland Park cop. I called him at his latest place of employment, and he agreed to speak with me the following week. He didn't immediately recall the case, but he thought it sounded like a "double" he investigated, in which the victims had their hearts cut out. This was an ex-cop alright. After sending a fax version of the investigator's report that had his name signed to it, I called him back. He did remember the case. He and Paul Lee had been on call during the morning when the murders were reported. It was a time when cops had plenty of work to keep them busy in the few neighborhoods that made up Highland Park. He remembered thinking that the Goines and Sailor killings were a result of drug involvement.

"We figured it was kind of dope-related," he said. "We had quite a bit of that back then. Our precinct was only about four square miles and we were getting like sixty homicides a year." About twenty-five of those murders—more than a third—Quinn said, were connected with drugs. Cortland, which extended directly west from near the front of Highland Park's municipal complex, was no rougher than any of the other surrounding streets, though it was apparently a place where residents preferred to mind their own business. All of the people living at the address of the incident were interviewed, but Quinn suspected they were afraid to speak up. There was no indication of silencers on the two .38s left at the scene. Which means that, even having heard no less than ten gunshots inside the house, if anyone at 232 Cortland knew, they weren't sharing it. Quinn recalled no signs of forced entry at the apartment. The killer or killers—he wasn't willing to guess at the number—were people known or recognized by the victims, he told me. The dazed children had already been removed from the house by the time Quinn and Detective Lee arrived.

"The children weren't able to give any information whatsoever," Quinn recalled. Police were left with no eyewitnesses and no physical evidence, and found no fingerprints on the weapons. And by the condition in which he found their bodies, Quinn estimated that Mr. Goines and Shirley Sailor had been dead for at least ten hours, leaving time for the suspects to put hundreds or thousands of miles between themselves and the crime, depending upon their mode of travel. Ultimately, Highland Park cops would find little to investigate beyond the initial police report to which Quinn signed his name. Without ever identifying a single suspect to question and without making a single arrest, the case that was one of only three double murders he would be assigned was placed in the inactive file.

"Right now, you would have to have almost a confession from whoever did it," Quinn told me before we ended our call. But Ciccone had disagreed, telling me: "Crimes have been solved with less evidence than this."

Highland Park, in 2003, is a vastly different place than it was, not quite thirty years earlier in 1974. The McGregor Library, where I wanted to do research, is closed to the public. The tiny city hall building that faces Woodward Avenue functions with few staff members. Hours of business are not the nine-to-five time frame that one might expect. Show up on the wrong day or at the wrong time, and you may not even gain entrance through the glass doors. What's left of the Highland Park Police Department operates out of a cramped police mini station near the center of a strip mall less than half a mile away. The Farmer Jack supermarket and the Ashley Stewart clothing store draw more activity and attention since the number of officers on the force has been drastically reduced, to the point where the handful of remaining cops are limited in the calls to which they can respond. Even the mayor has faded into relative obscurity, affected by various stresses and with his authority limited by the state powers enforced with his support. Highland Park is a city in decline. Millions of dollars in debt are largely to blame. There has been talk, in the past year or longer, of making the city a part of Detroit's municipal domain. Also discussed was the possibility of a complete takeover by the Michigan government.

Cortland Avenue might be viewed as one example of the need for such an intervention. The short stretch that begins at Woodward and runs through to Second Avenue is not terribly different from other sections of the city, or from many in neighboring Detroit, but this makes for sad commentary. It's only by the comparison to worse blocks that this stretch of Cortland is able to emerge as less depressing in appearance. There is a row of out-wardly well-kept and decent houses, which look as if they've prob-ably been occupied for a long while. After all, this isn't the sort of neighborhood that beckons new residents. A little farther down there is the sudden manifestation of empty lots. Another set of houses that appears on the opposite side is a striking contradiction. Abandoned and literally crumbling, they have the look of easy ac-cess for vagrancy or other illegal occupancy. On the opposite side of the street are two schools within short distance of one another. Cortland Elementary is the smaller of them and the closest to the spot that I'm seeking. There is extremely short, winter-bleached grass near the street, but it grows tall and thick deeper into the lot, which has obviously not been tended. There is no more 232 Cort-land. The building where Mr. Goines and Shirley Sailor were mur-dered is gone without a trace. A passerby might not even be aware that there used to be a residence in the barren location. Any mem-ory of Mr. Goines is imperceptible.

A 1987 *Detroit News* article included the frequently used head-shot of the author, tight-lipped and expressionless, above the cap-tion "Donald Goines: He lived, wrote and, at age 35, died by the streets." Along with the incorrect age at death that it listed, the feature included at least three or four other mischaracterizations, such as an improper count of fourteen books that "still sell," when the total of Mr. Goines's titles was sixteen, and its offhanded label-ing of Black Bottom as "a ghetto in Detroit." Significant, however, were a few of the quotes. Pete Locke, identified as an executive editor with Holloway House, told the *News*: "Each generation is reading him. We still get fan letters each month from kids who don't realize he's dead." Myrtle Goines, then seventy-seven, was reported to have contradicted the most commonly held beliefs about the events that led to her son's writing career. Mrs. Goines appeared to tell the paper that he began *Dopefiend* way back in 1965, before Holloway House published Iceberg Slim's first book, which would have made it improbable that he could have been Mr. Goines's inspiration. Possibly, his mother had just lost some of her recollection, because she was quoted in a way that suggested

Mr. Goines got into pimping after he started to write during a jail sentence. "When he got out I told him to keep writing," she was quoted as saying. "I told him he could make some money one day. But he wanted to make it fast." Most intriguing was Joan Coney's quote about her brother. While she and her sister seemed much less certain about who they felt killed Mr. Goines at the times when I interviewed them, the *News* article read: "Goines captured the life of the ghetto so vividly it cost him his life, says his sister, Joan Coney, 38. 'The characters in his book resembled those in real life,' she says, 'so they killed him.'"

Ralph Watts, the brother-in-law to Shirley Sailor—who accompanied Mr. Goines to the dealer's house a few nights before the murders—repeated Ms. Coney's assertion. He didn't specifically place the man they went to visit that evening in any of Mr. Goines's books, but he recalled that the pusher's name was Ronnie. He recognized what he believed may have been a major clue about who committed the homicides when, days after the murders, one of the children began to announce, "Ronnie killed my Shirley! Ronnie killed my Shirley!" Some of the women in the family quickly shut the little one's mouth, and this information was never reported to police, for fear that the child might be put in danger. But whether or not the dealer called Ronnie had seen resemblance of himself in any novel, others agreed with former detective Quinn's suggestion that the crimes were simply drug-related, having nothing to do with what Mr. Goines wrote.

Still, there was another, more unsettling version reported among Sailor family members: that the words of the little girl who turned four years old days after the killings implicated cops who were allegedly there before detectives arrived at the scene. The same daughter who Watts remembered calling Ronnie's name said that uniformed officers—or at least two men dressed like them—shot Mr. Goines while he sat at the typewriter, and turned on Sailor when she screamed. As one Sailor sibling remembers it, the child broke a week of complete silence by telling how murderers then hid her and toddler Donna in the bathroom, explaining, "We don't kill little girls." The problem with this account is that there's no reference, in any of the documentation I gathered, to Mr. Goines being found at or near a typewriter. It may, however, explain origins of the dramatic rumor his admirers would repeat for decades to come. Moreover, it raises questions about whether an author who occasionally wrote about dirty cops could have died because of it.

In the early part of 2003, I found Walter Williamson occupying the same north Detroit neighborhood where he and his family had lived throughout the years. He had recently left his home in Westland, Michigan, to move in with his mother and care for her before she died. Walter was planning to return to Westland before the year's end. With no telephone number available, Charles Glover and I drove to his address, hoping to talk with him. I was told that he hadn't publicly spoken about Mr. Goines in almost thirty years. Charles suggested we bring along a chess board and a bottle of wine. After looking out onto the porch and seeing Charles, Walter opened the door. He looked nothing like the timid, little man I imagined who had been frightened into silence by his friend's murder. Instead, Walter showed outward signs of the player he had been in his prime. Wearing a bathrobe and hairnet, with a thick and plentiful amount of straightened black tresses netted and bundled upward onto his head, he looked at least ten years younger than the age he claimed, seventy-two. I was surprised at how quickly he appeared to recognize Charles, who credited his uncle and his uncle's companions like Walter with helping to give him a sense of manhood, in spite of their unorthodox and corruptive influence.

The first thing I noticed after shaking Walter's hand and being shown into his living room was a chess set with all of its pieces in position sitting on a green fold-up table. The set I'd brought wouldn't be needed. After at least four decades, Walter was still a passionate chess player. He was expecting a friend to arrive for their regular game any minute. My bottle of wine wouldn't be opened, either. As we all sat down, Walter told us he had stopped drinking and smoking. He was in recovery from treatment for prostate cancer and had only been outside the house three times during the previous two months. He had been through a rough time and was still in the midst of a slow recovery process, he told us. If we wanted to get older, he said, we should pay specific attention to our health now. Was this the sort of talk that retired pimps and Hall of Fame players normally delivered? When his chess opponent arrived, the flashes and flourishes that Charles remembered began.

"I'm glad you came. You know why?" Walter asked the younger man who sat across the board from him. "I ain't kicked nobody's ass today." We all laughed. That sounded more like player talk to me. Walter had switched his TV set to an audio jazz channel, and in no time we were listening to mellow tunes as cigarette smoke filled the small living room. Charles said it was just like he remembered things when his uncle was alive, except, of course, that Walter wasn't smoking. When Walter's visitor learned that Charles and I were there to do discuss Walter's memories of Mr. Goines, he seemed surprised.

"The author?" he asked in disbelief. The man revealed a subtle reverence that I had recognized in the voices of any number of people I asked about Mr. Goines's books on other occasions. Walter's partner had never accepted the stories he heard about the longtime friendship. "I thought that was just Walt talkin' shit," he said. Walter had missed his old friend over the years. He and Mr. Goines had been as thick as thieves in the literal sense. Listening to him speak of the many times they shared, it was easy to imagine the writer sitting across from him at the chess board where his visitor sat. Mr. Goines had left behind no interviews that I ever came across. Most likely, he had never received an opportunity to give any formal Q and A. And I found myself wondering, from time to time, just what he might say if he were alive and able to talk to me about his life. Would he have overcome his addiction? Would he have continued writing? Walter's recollections were to be the final contribution I received from those who personally knew Mr. Goines's traits and ways. Yet, not even the people who took the time to talk with me were prepared to say what the man might have become. Walter only knew that his friend had genuine potential. His most pensive moments appeared at the times when he thought about the sudden way in which the author died.

"It was horrible because Donnie had a name," he said. I knew he hadn't meant to suggest that the death of anyone less known would have been less significant. Mr. Goines's popularity only made the blow of his sudden absence even more devastating. Walter had been excited to see how far his running buddy might go and how much he might achieve.

Talking about Mr. Goines's death took him back to that day just weeks before the murders. There seemed to be no doubt in Walter's mind that he had been in the presence of the men who fired the bullets. All three were uncommonly tall, at least six feet five inches, he thought. They were Caucasians with stringy hair and rotting teeth. They wore jeans, and by Walter's assessment, they were probably addicts like Mr. Goines. The men didn't necessarily give Walter the impression that they were directly affected by the dirty trick Mr. Goines said he had pulled, whatever it was. They seemed like men who came in from out of town to do a job, and who were vicious enough in their motivation to see it through. There was dope involved with their reason for coming to 232 Cortland on that day. Mr. Goines had acknowledged he "put shit on" someone. Walter speculated that Mr. Goines might have been given access to heroin on consignment before he left L.A. and failed to settle his debt. Out of fear, Walter had deliberately remained silent when he got the opportunity to speak to police about what he remembered. He couldn't be certain that the men he thought to be his friend's killers were not still in town. It wasn't until later, he told me, when he described them to a person who was working on another project about Mr. Goines. But Walter wasn't clear on how much time had passed since the killings and when he received this telephone call.

One or two who were less connected to Mr. Goines's personal life, however, thought the drug connection to Mr. Goines's murder was a shaky one. The field trip I thought it was absolutely necessary that I take was to Los Angeles. Although his experiences in the city comprised a relatively small and mostly unpleasant chapter in his own life, aside from Detroit, L.A. was the primary setting for Mr. Goines's novels. It was also the place where I could have a face-to-face interview with Bentley Morriss, the man largely responsible for bringing Donald Goines's books, along with the first biography about his life, to the world's attention. Originally printed the same year of its subject's murder, *Donald Writes No More* was written by Eddie Stone. I didn't miss the coincidence that I was the second person of the same first name to examine Mr. Goines's life. I remember flipping through *Donald Writes No More* once or twice at the bookstore and thinking it was rather flat but forming no real conclusion otherwise. I only questioned how thorough the research could have been, given that there were only weeks between the time of Mr. Goines's and Shirley Sailor's deaths and the publication's date of copyright. (In what I thought a frightening peculiarity, my sister later read to me, from its third or fourth page, the most peculiar disclaimer for a so-called biography that I had ever heard and eventually saw for myself: "Some characters, places and incidents are either the product of the author's imagination or used fictitiously. Any resemblance to actual events or locales or persons, living or dead, is entirely coincidental.") On the other hand, while I considered that I was at the disadvantage of working on a book close to three decades later, I waited for some of the personal records I requested for months at a time. In fact, I was finished with all my writing for the manuscript, when, after nearly a year, I still hadn't received the DD 214 Air Force file of Mr. Goines's military history.

I had heard stories about Bentley Morriss and his handling of business related to the Goines estate. A few family members felt that, with all their loved one had contributed—and was still contributing—to the success of Holloway House, they deserved more than the periodic royalty payments they were given. Whether this was true or false, I wanted to get his perspectives and check out the headquarters of the place that now billed itself "World's Largest Publisher of Black Experience Paperback Books," due, of course in large part, to Mr. Goines's body of work. I first talked with Mr. Morriss on the telephone. He seemed a friendly man with the speaking voice of a radio announcer. In June 2001, he wrote to me and was nice enough to send along a press kit and a copy of *Street Players*. I had heard about one or two film projects that were to be based on Goines books. One had even been pitched on a cable television channel. It aired a commercial for the soundtrack to *Black Gangster*, a movie that would be based on the novel. But it turned out there were seven more books, for which there were movie options, at least one that was reportedly in the postproduction, or final, stages of actual filming. Companies in New York and California had expressed interest in bringing *Never Die Alone*, *Daddy Cool*, *Crime Partners*, *Black Girl Lost*, *Death List*, *Kenyatta's Revenge* and *Kenyatta's Last Hit* to the big screen, Morriss informed me.

"Practically all his books have been translated into French," he also wrote. "His books are sold throughout the globe, and in the past twenty-five years have never been out of print. The hip-hop and rap generation [of] artists have embraced his works, and sales increase each year with a whole new generation of readers." It was just a little less than a year from the day I received his letter when I got out of bed at 5:00 A.M. with plans to meet him in the afternoon. Including plenty of layover time, it was a long trip to L.A. From our two or three telephone conversations, I envisioned a stocky, energetic man with white hair that contrasted deeply tanned skin. A prototypical, semiretired, California-beach type is what I expected, but all I was right about was the white hair. After catching a private taxi to Holloway House, I went into the lobby and took the elevator up to its editorial section. I waited with a receptionist until I was called back into his office. Morriss, seated at a large, wood-finish desk, was not outwardly the California-slick businessman at all. If he spent significant time in the sun, his complexion gave no indication. His attire was a simple department-store dress shirt and buttoned casual sweater with slacks.

Following a handshake, I sat in one of the comfortable chairs of his spacious office. I thanked him for taking the time to talk with me and started my micro cassette recorder. Within the first fifteen minutes of the interview, Morriss offered an anecdote. He recalled an encounter at a gathering of a professional organization about ten, maybe fifteen, years ago. A black woman of about sixty approached him at the Holloway House exhibit during the conference.

"We were exhibiting at the American Library Association," he said, "and these were all people of 'very high intellectual capability,' and here we are with Iceberg Slim and Donald Goines and the rest of them, and, you know, some hard-rock literature, and a lovely looking lady, small, diminutive, *very* well-dressed came up and said—and we had, also the other series, we had the Mankind books, which are autobiographies of African Americans that have made grade achievement. We have about sixty of those that we've done. And she looked at them and she said, 'This is lovely, but how can you publish material like *this*?' And I said, 'Ma'am, have you read Donald Goines and Iceberg Slim?' She says, 'Absolutely. Every single one of them.' So that kind of gave me an indication, or should give you an indication, that there may be a group or a class within the community that says this is 'street stuff' but privately appreciates it, nonetheless."

Morriss and his staff came up with in-house theories about who killed Mr. Goines and Shirley Sailor that resembled the speculation shared by friends and relatives: "We couldn't believe it. We got a call, I think from one of the sisters, who then sent us tearsheets from the *Detroit Free Press*. We called everybody we knew in Detroit. Could they verify it? Did this really happen, and was there any lead as to who did it? But there was no additional information. There were two theories—and they were strictly theories. One, he wrote about the life that he knew. He wrote about the people he knew, people that had crossed his path, and one theory is that if he continued writing about these people, they could be identified. And if they could be identified, they might expose themselves to arrest. The other theory, which doesn't make any sense to me, is that he had built up such a big tag with his supplier that they were angry, but that's ridiculous. I mean you can break his leg or poke an eye out, but you don't kill your source. You know then you're not gonna get paid. He's gone."

Mr. Goines's goal of taking his stories to a film studio appeared to be materializing at the time I spoke with Morriss. *Crime Partners*, which starred rap recording artists including Snoop Dogg and Ja Rule, was distributed in home-film release. "The other books are in option, film option," Morriss said, "and if you know anything about film option—in this town, there's about maybe 30,000 film options a year, and less than one-tenth of one percent ultimately become a film."

"Oh, so that's not such a big deal, in other words?" I asked him.

"Well it is to us because they pay option money," he explained. "They protect it [for their use]. They give you X amount of money. You sign a contract. Then if they need an extension, they pay additional money and so on. So no, it's pretty good for us."

The following summer of 2003, Morriss would tell me he planned to attend a "rough cut" screening of the *Never Die Alone* film adaptation starring rapper DMX.

Of any suggestions that Mr. Goines was unhappy with his publishing agreements Morriss said he was not aware. "He never said to us that if you don't give me more money, or if you don't promote it more, then I'm gonna go elsewhere. We never had that kind of a conversation." Yet, while he said the writer never complained to him about finances, it struck Morriss as interesting that he was later contacted by Mr. Goines's old friend, Al Clark, who reportedly sought more compensation than what the author left for him in the will. "He even, at one time, contended that he wrote the books," added Morriss. "It wasn't true. It just wasn't true. I got a call from him one day, and I said, 'Mr. Clark, whatever you feel is right, put it in a letter to me. Send it to me, and we'll investigate the best we can.' Never heard from him." By 2002, Holloway House had sold an estimated 5 million books written by Donald Goines.

One of the things that troubled me the entire time I was writing and researching this man's life was the way he left home as a boy. There seemed no rational motivation for his wanting to go through the trouble of faking his age, joining the air force, and serving for the time that he did, apparently without ever revealing the truth. Particularly considering that it was wartime, a boy his age should have preferred to be nearly anyplace else but in a uniform. Being flown to Korea was a tremendous leap from watching old combat movies and playing with toy guns. I thought the question of why a kid who got into card gambling and thievery would be willing to adjust to military discipline was also worth contemplating. I've been a peer as well as a mentor to adolescent boys who showed behavioral problems, and not one of them ever expressed a desire to join the armed services. Not one. It stands to reason that Mr. Goines was, at least, somewhat familiar with the rigidity of military culture before he decided to join up. At least one of his acquaintances, Walter, had gone to Korea before he was sent there. Any impressions he received about survival in the air force had to indicate the required adjustment to regulations and restrictions, and it's hard to imagine that he would have found this appealing. So whatever it was that possessed him to leave behind the material comforts and security of a middle-class childhood must have been excruciatingly stressful. Marie Richardson, the only living witness to what took place inside the Goines home during that period, told me repeatedly that she just didn't know. Maybe her brother was just "bad," she said at one point. But, considering that he returned from Asia a heroin addict, as far as I was concerned, there had to be a more revealing explanation of what had driven him there. When I spoke to historian Paul Lee about this, he cautioned me not to "look for easy answers." In the research seminars he presents through his independent company, Best Efforts, Inc., he repeats a basic rule: Avoid assumptions; the truth is often hidden behind them. So if I couldn't assume that anything in his personal life had been the cause of his running far away, what else did I have? I contacted Dr. Kenneth Cole to try and get some professional feedback.

Cole is a Los Angeles–based psychologist and author of the children's book *Good News*. His work has brought him into contact with youth who are the products of urban environments that were even less conducive to their maturity and healthy development than the immediate surroundings in Mr. Goines's childhood. A native of Flint, Michigan, one of Mr. Goines's various stomping grounds, Cole was immediately struck by the color issues Mr. Goines experienced as a boy.

"One thing that did come out, initially, was his whole perception of himself as a black man," Cole said. "If someone is insecure about himself as a black man, one of the things he may do is embrace things that he perceives as representing black culture." It had struck me as fairly obvious that Mr. Goines fell in with the wrong crowd as part of a childish reach toward social acceptance. Plenty of young people still make that mistake. What I hadn't considered was that self-consciousness about his physical appearance and related insecurity may have been at the very core of his emotional issues. Both of Mr. Goines's sisters had suggested this once or twice, but it struck me as an oversimplified explanation. I knew that, tragically, teenagers had killed themselves and, in more recent years, others as a result of feeling socially outcast. Yet, according to Dr. Cole's insights, Mr. Goines may have made the majority of his unfortunate choices based on the perceptions he developed as an adolescent. I thought the attention he later received from women must have remedied the early discomfort about his looks. In fact, Ms. Coney told me about memories of her brother in moments of vanity, when he would stand in front of a mirror and pinch his own behind. But I'm aware that we don't always see in ourselves what others see in us. Underneath it all, Mr. Goines was both sensitive and human, so he was not an exception to this truth. His immersion in crime and drug abuse, Dr. Cole explained, could have been an early response to his misinterpretation of how black men should think and act. Harder to determine was the reason he left home as a teenager. Whether or not he experienced some form of abuse, as I'd heard, Cole noted a behavior pattern that seemed to follow Mr. Goines into his adult years: "It seemed that much of what he was doing was far extreme. His books are *extreme* extreme, and that's good."

Mr. Goines's sense of displacement may have begun in his family, Dr. Cole added. "He really was the odd man out, from the get-go. He just never really seemed to fit in." The psychologist pointed out that, notwithstanding the provisions of his childhood, Mr. Goines may have seen his family's social status and his role as the only son as a source of pressure, rather than privilege. He surely was not the first child who chose a different direction, despite a parent's desire to share an inheritance.

"You could almost wonder, given that he was able to write a bunch of books in a short time—and high on heroin while he did it—there was a possibility that he could have been a pretty gifted kid," Cole said. He suggested to me the possibility that Mr. Goines's poor grades and apparent disinterest in school was related to a learning disorder, such as dyslexia, a point Marie Richardson once raised in reference to her brother. The psychologist dismissed the idea Mr. Goines expressed in his "Private Thoughts" letter that he couldn't write without heroin as "junkie logic," no more than the typical indication of drug dependency. This would have suggested that Mr. Goines was genetically predisposed to becoming a heroin addict.

With a little more guidance, if not from his parents, maybe from a neighbor, priest, or counselor, Cole said, Mr. Goines may have committed himself to another course. But Cole sees the novelist's achievements as remarkable, nonetheless: "What does it say that in the midst of heroin addiction, and a lifestyle in which he sort of compromised his soul, that he was able to find some sense of purpose?"

The psychologist's assessment of Mr. Goines's writing reflected his view that all presentations of American culture are relevant. Dr. Cole's comment resembled a quote from the European publication *La Liberte' de l'Est*: "What is great about Goines is that you feel you've become more intelligent once you have read his stories of pain and grief. His stories almost have an ethnographic value."

The more painful and violent elements of the Donald Goines legacy struck on the morning of March 28, 1992. Mr. Goines's namesake, a grandchild by his son, was one of three people to be murdered in nearly a week filled with Detroit tragedies. A *Detroit News* story bearing the headline "Another child, 2 adults killed" appeared on the front page of the paper with a photograph of the three-year-old beneath the words. "Donald Goines III became the sixth Detroit child slain in six days when someone opened fire about 3:30 A.M. on the 9200 block of Grandville, police said," the story detailed. "Also killed were Donald's godmother, Tanya Smith, 24, and an unidentified 26-year-old man. Smith's boyfriend, Earl Sheppard, 26, and an unidentified 24-year-old woman, were wounded. Witnesses and relatives said the boy and four adults were in a car in the driveway of a home owned by Smith and Sheppard when someone opened fire. The car lurched forward, breaking through the driveway gate and coming to rest in the backyard." Police had no immediate suspects or motive in the shootings. The child's parents, Donald II and Latonya Williams, were at home when the incident took place. It wasn't long, however, before the horrible news reached his father, and Donald II informed his mother, who carried a photo of her grandbaby in her purse. "My son called," Thelma Powell (formerly Thelma Howard) told the paper. "He said, 'The baby is dead.' I don't think I can remember another thing he told me." As in the Goines and Sailor killings, according to Detroit police, no one was ever arrested for these crimes.

In an unrelated episode, one of Mr. Goines's younger relatives was shot several times as he traveled a low road to fame and financial comfort reminiscent of one Mr. Goines had once tested. Apparently, he was attacked as a result of his affiliation with a flamboyant Detroit drug dealer called "White Boy Rick," who gained a considerable profile in the 1990s. The young man later relocated and began following in the footsteps of the author and a few other Goines men who had begun careers in the media.

What will likely be the most lasting impact of Mr. Goines's writing, however, extends beyond any of his relatives and descendants. It will be the realism with which he captured and portrayed the struggles and small, occasional victories of those who encountered the most tempting and often difficult challenges of being people of color in urban America. Rap artists, such as Nas, who recorded the lyrics "My life is like a Donald Goines novel" for a 1997 song, filmmakers like John Singleton, and thousands of teenagers, many of whom are still discovering Mr. Goines's work, strive to duplicate his authenticity. They strive to display the swagger of Earl the Pearl, the cunning of Eldorado Red, the fearlessness of Kenyatta. College-course instructors and admirers, such as Robert Skinner, point to Mr. Goines's writing as creativity with a great deal more depth than what was attributed to it during his brief career.

"I think it's safe to say that any discussion of noir fiction or the

African-American crime story is incomplete without including Goines," says Skinner, an author and librarian at Xavier University in New Orleans. Skinner says Mr. Goines's close identification with the concerns and struggles of his characters is apparent.

"There's no book that I've read that illustrates this better than *Daddy Cool*," he continues, "which I understand is an important cult favorite in Europe, where Goines . . . still has a considerable audience. *Daddy Cool* is a real urban tragedy in which concepts of 'love' are twisted by the environment. That Daddy Cool is killed at the end of the story isn't the ultimate tragedy—it's the fact that the one person in the world that he loves unreservedly, his daughter, is so corrupted by the pimp she falls in love with that she turns on her father and protector.

"There's a great deal more that can be said about Goines. I think he continues to have an audience among African-Americans because he has created strong, black protagonists who have risen above white oppression in the only way they can, and who control their own destinies within a hostile environment."

At Detroit Memorial, I find myself the only visitor a short time before its attendants close their gates to the public on a Thursday afternoon. When I arrive, I quickly navigate the circular paths that lead to my target area. I'm looking for Section 38, Marker No. 2014. But I've chosen a bad day to look for Mr. Goines's burial site, and there probably won't be any good days until the spring begins and the weather breaks. Hardened snow crunches under my feet as I walk through the empty cemetery. I look carefully, but nearly the entire ground is covered. Across the expansive acres, artificial flowers and wreaths laid at grave sites blast a colorful contrast against the snow. The striking difference between death and life is apparent in the complete stillness of my surroundings, where birds chirping is the only recognizable sound. I pace in various directions around Section 38, finding no signs of grass and not knowing whether the stiff areas that I step on are headstones or sheets of ice. I kick randomly at spots that I have a weak hunch might be the marker I need. At one point, I stop and wait, feeling that I may be psychically led to the site, but it doesn't happen. I take a last look around, attempting to absorb some energetic vibration. Then I see a car that I believe has been sent to search the grounds for people like me before the cemetery closes. At this point, I know I have to leave. I crunch my way back through the snow, feeling a little disappointed but not discouraged. Wherever the particular spot may be, I know Mr. Goines's remains are at rest. I hope the same can be said for his weary spirit. I get into my truck and drive past the tall monuments and religious idols toward Detroit Memorial's gates. It hasn't been such an unsettling visit. I'll be back again one day.

Notes on Sources

In addition to personal interviews, vital records, government documents, historical reference publications, and Donald Goines's novels, news clippings, personal notes, and data from three electronic World Wide Web sites were used to support the assertions of this biography. Sources are listed chronologically and indicated with attribution.

Preface
—Donald Goines, *Dopefiend* (Los Angeles: Holloway House, 1971): character and plot descriptions.
—Peter Gavrilovich and Bill McGraw, eds., *The Detroit Almanac: 300 Years of Life in the Motor City* (Detroit: Detroit Free Press, 2001): most Detroit-specific history.

Prelude: Death in Retrospect
—Interviews with Charles Glover, Marie Richardson, and Joan Coney, 1999–2000.

Maturing
—Interview with Robin Ussery: quoted material.
—Interview with Marie Richardson, 2001: Evanston 1934 recount and early Goines/Baugh family information.

—Pulaski County Certificate of Marriage: George Baugh/Clairette Ford.

—Interviews with Lynda Crist, Jefferson Davis Papers Project, and William Cooper Jr., author of *Jefferson Davis, American* (New York: Knopf, 2001), 2002: background on Davis estate and slave ownership.

—Interview with Betty Dooley, 2002: Little Rock farming information.

—U.S. 1910 Census: Baugh residence data.

—C. Vann Woodward, *The Strange Career of Jim Crow*, third edition (New York: Oxford University Press, 1974): lynching, mob violence, and most race-discrimination background before 1970.

—Kareem Abdul-Jabbar and Alan Steinberg, *Black Profiles in Courage: A Legacy of African-American Achievement* (New York: Avon Books, 1996): Brownsville episode and supplemental information about southern racist incidents.

—State of Michigan Certificate of Live Birth: Donald Goines's birth information.

—Peter Gavrilovich and Bill McGraw, eds., *The Detroit Almanac: 300 Years of Life in the Motor City* (Detroit: Detroit Free Press, 2001): most Detroit-specific history.

—Interview with Roman Godzak, Catholic Diocese, 2002: Catholic schools background.

—Catholic Diocese academic transcript: Donald Goines's admission date, records.

—Detroit Board of Education academic transcript: Donald Goines's public schools, courses, and grades.

War

—Donald Goines, *Whoreson* (Los Angeles: Holloway House, 1972): quoted material.

—Peter Gavrilovich and Bill McGraw, eds., *The Detroit Almanac: 300 Years of Life in the Motor City* (Detroit: Detroit Free Press, 2001): most Detroit-specific history.

—David Lee Poremba, *Detroit: A Motor City History* (Charleston: Arcadia, 2002): supplemental Detroit history.

—"Minnie the Moocher," performed by Cab Calloway: quoted material.

—Interview with Marie Richardson: quoted material and family background information.

—Detroit Board of Education academic transcript: Donald Goines's public schools, courses, and grades.

—C. Vann Woodward, *The Strange Career of Jim Crow*, third edition (New York: Oxford University Press, 1974): lynching, mob violence, and most race-discrimination background before 1970.

—Kwame Anthony Appiah and Henry Louis Gates, Jr., eds., *Africana: The Encyclopedia of the African and African American Experience* (Boston: Basic Civitas

Books, 1999): most background on nationally and internationally known historical figures, events, and institutions.

Dope Fiend

—Interview with Paul Lee: quoted material.

—Joan Coney, with Marie Richardson and Charles Glover, "Memories of a Street Writer," unpublished writings: recount of Donald Goines's return from the military; his use of heroin; writing career; and relationships with women, sons, and daughters.

—Interview with Marie Richardson and Joan Coney: recollections of their parents and brother.

—Peter Gavrilovich and Bill McGraw, eds., *The Detroit Almanac: 300 Years of Life in the Motor City* (Detroit: Detroit Free Press, 2001): most Detroit-specific history.

—C. Vann Woodward, *The Strange Career of Jim Crow*, third edition (New York: Oxford University Press, 1974): lynching, mob violence, and most race-discrimination background before 1970.

—Melba Pattillo Beals, *Warriors Don't Cry* (New York: Pocket Books, 1994): Central High School episode and quoted material.

—Interview with William Shackleford, Federal Bureau of Investigation, 2002: "white slavery" file information.

Cash and Bitches

—Donald Goines, *Daddy Cool* (Los Angeles: Holloway House, 1974): quoted material.

—Interview with Sam Greenlee, 2002, and *Hoodlum* motion picture Website: supplemental information about policy/numbers hustle.

—Interview with Charles Glover, 1999: Temptations, trunk prisoner, canary, and boosting anecdotes.

—Recorder's Court, City of Detroit court records: information about Goines, Hawkins, Higgins crimes and sentencing.

—U.S. Court of Appeals for the Sixth Circuit records: information about Goines and Stewart crimes and sentencing.

—Peter Gavrilovich and Bill McGraw, eds., *The Detroit Almanac: 300 Years of Life in the Motor City* (Detroit: Detroit Free Press, 2001): most Detroit-specific history.

—Elaine Latzman Moon, comp., *Untold Tales, Unsung Heroes: An Oral History of Detroit's African American Community 1918–1967* (Detroit: Wayne State University Press, 1993): Romney recount of response to 1967 rebellion.

The Joint

—Donald Goines, *White Man's Justice, Black Man's Grief* (Los Angeles: Holloway House, 1973): quoted material.

—Peter Gavrilovich and Bill McGraw, eds., *The Detroit Almanac: 300 Years of Life in the Motor City* (Detroit: Detroit Free Press, 2001): most Detroit-specific history.

—*Random House College Dictionary:* Terre Haute history.

—Terre Haute U.S. Prison public affairs office: size of facility.

—Letter from Marie Richardson to Donald Goines, date unknown: quoted material.

—Donald Goines's prison vocabulary test: quoted material.

—Kwame Anthony Appiah and Henry Louis Gates, Jr., eds., *Africana: The Encyclopedia of the African and African American Experience* (Boston: Basic Civitas Books, 1999): most background on nationally and internationally known historical figures, events, and institutions.

—Joe Louis Moore, *The Legacy of the Panthers: A Photographic Exhibition* (Berkeley: The Dr. Huey P. Newton Foundation/Inkworks Press, 1995): supplemental information about the Black Panthers.

—C. Vann Woodward, *The Strange Career of Jim Crow,* third edition (New York: Oxford University Press, 1974): lynching, mob violence, and most race-discrimination background before 1970.

—Interview with Eddie B. Allen Sr, 2002: background on Hanoi Hannah.

—Interview with Bill Thomas, 2002: background on conscientious objection.

—Michigan Department of Corrections record, received 8/15/69: inmate information.

—Interview with Marie Richardson and Joan Coney: recollections of their brother.

—World Wide Web posting of 1973 *Los Angeles Free Press* interview: quoted Iceberg Slim material.

—Handwritten manuscript pages for the book *Whoreson*: quoted material.

—Letter from Mildred Pruett, dated Nov. 4, 1969: quoted material.

Publisher

—Undated personal note: quoted material.

—S. Torriano Berry with Venise T. Berry, *The 50 Most Influential Black Films: A Celebration of African-American Talent, Determination, and Creativity* (New York: Citadel Press, 2001): 1970s film background.

—Interview with Bentley Morriss, June 2002: background on Iceberg Slim and Holloway House.

—Eldridge Cleaver, *Soul on Ice* (New York: Dell Publishing, 1968): quoted material.

—Robert Beck, *Pimp* (Los Angeles: Holloway House, 1967): quoted material.

—Interview with Paul Lee, 2002: observed Breitman lawsuit paperwork housed at the Tamiment Library, New York.

—Joan Coney, with Marie Richardson and Charles Glover, "Memories of a Street Writer," unpublished writings: recount of Donald Goines's return from the military; his use of heroin; writing career; and relationships with women, sons, and daughters.

—Donald Goines, *Dopefiend* (Los Angeles: Holloway House, 1971): quoted material.

—Letter from unidentified Holloway House editor, December 29, 1970.

—Holloway House writer's agreement: quoted material.

West Coast

—Interview with Robert Skinner: quoted material.

—Peter Gavrilovich and Bill McGraw, eds., *The Detroit Almanac: 300 Years of Life in the Motor City* (Detroit: Detroit Free Press, 2001): most Detroit-specific history.

—Kwame Anthony Appiah and Henry Louis Gates, Jr., eds., *Africana: The Encyclopedia of the African and African American Experience* (Boston: Basic Civitas Books, 1999): most background on nationally and internationally known historical figures, events, and institutions.

—Interview with Marie Teasley, 2002: recount of meeting with Donald Goines at *Michigan Chronicle*.

—Joan Coney, with Marie Richardson and Charles Glover, "Memories of a Street Writer," unpublished writings: recount of Donald Goines's return from military; his use of heroin; writing career; and relationships with women, sons, and daughters.

—Interview with Raymond Stevens, 2001: background on Shorty Hunt and neighborhood.

—Donald Goines, *Whoreson* (Los Angeles: Holloway House, 1972): excerpted material.

—Donald Goines, *Kenyatta's Last Hit* (Los Angeles: Holloway House, 1975): Myrtle Goines's dedication.

—Donald Goines, *Black Gangster* (Los Angeles: Holloway House, 1972): plot and character description.

—Interview with Ralph Watts, 2002: background of Sailor family.

—S. Torriano Berry with Venise T. Berry, *The 50 Most Influential Black Films: A Celebration of African-American Talent, Determination, and Creativity* (New York: Citadel Press, 2001): 1970s film background.

—PBS television Web posting: background on zoot-suit conflict.

—Interview with Bentley Morriss, June 2002: recount of Donald Goines's arrival and experience living in L.A.

—Undated letter to potential publisher: excerpted material.

—"Private Thoughts," letter dated September 1, 1973: excerpted material.

—Undated personal note: quoted material.

Prodigal Son

—Donald Goines, *Never Die Alone* (Los Angeles: Holloway House, 1974): quoted material.

—Undated personal note: quoted material.

—Interview with Walter Williamson, 2003: recount of Donald Goines's return from L.A.

—Donald Goines, *Street Players* (Los Angeles: Holloway House, 1973): plot and character descriptions.

—Donald Goines, *White Man's Justice, Black Man's Grief* (Los Angeles: Holloway House, 1973): quoted material.

—Donald Goines, *Black Girl Lost* (Los Angeles: Holloway House, 1973): plot and character descriptions.

—Donald Goines, *Eldorado Red* (Los Angeles: Holloway House, 1974): plot and character descriptions.

—Kwame Anthony Appiah and Henry Louis Gates, Jr., eds., *Africana: The Encyclopedia of the African and African American Experience* (Boston: Basic Civitas Books, 1999): most background on nationally and internationally known historical figures, events, and institutions.

—Undated personal note: quoted material.

—Peter Gavrilovich and Bill McGraw, eds., *The Detroit Almanac: 300 Years of Life in the Motor City* (Detroit: Detroit Free Press, 2001): most Detroit-specific history.

—Undated personal note: quoted material.

—Joan Coney, with Marie Richardson and Charles Glover, "Memories of a Street Writer," unpublished writings: recount of Donald Goines's return from the military; his use of heroin; writing career; and relationships with women, sons, and daughters.

—"Inner City Blues," performed by Marvin Gaye: quoted material.

—Donald Goines, *Inner City Hoodlum* (Los Angeles: Holloway House, 1975): plot and character descriptions.

—Last will and testament of Donald Goines, May 11, 1974: excerpted material.

—*Cry Revenge* and *Kenyatta's Escape*: book covers.

—Interview with Bentley Morriss, June 2002: quoted material.

—Donald Goines, *Swamp Man* (Los Angeles: Holloway House, 1974): excerpted material.

—Donald Goines, *Daddy Cool* (Los Angeles: Holloway House, 1974): quoted material.

—Undated personal note: quoted material.

—Donald Goines, *Dopefiend* (Los Angeles: Holloway House, 1971): quoted material.

—Donald Goines, *Crime Partners* (Los Angeles: Holloway House, 1974): quoted material.

—Donald Goines, *Death List* (Los Angeles: Holloway House, 1974): plot and characters.

—Donald Goines, *Never Die Alone* (Los Angeles: Holloway House, 1974): quoted material.

—Undated personal note: quoted material.

—Personal note, dated Oct. 18, [1974]: quoted material.

—Interview with Ralph Watts, 2002: recount of trip to see Ronnie.

—Interview with Joan Coney, 2002: recount of reaction to Donald Goines/Shirley Sailor murders.

—*Detroit News,* "Three Murdered in Highland Park," Oct. 23, 1974: quoted material.

—State of Michigan Certificate of Death, 1974: quoted material.

Legacy: An Epilogue

—Clippings from unidentified French newspapers: quoted material.

—Donald Goines, *Kenyatta's Last Hit* (Los Angeles: Holloway House, 1975): quoted material.

—Telephone interview with Bentley Morriss: recount of Carleton Hollander contribution.

—Letter to Marie Richardson from Seymour Fieg: quoted material.

—Chicago Reader article, November 15, 2002: quoted material.

—Highland Park Police investigative summaries: quoted material.

—Interview with Craig Ciccone: quoted material.

—Interview with Sgt. William McClain: recollections of Billy Quinn.

—Computer e-mail: quoted material.

—Interview with Billy Quinn: quoted material.

—*Detroit News* article dated March 1, 1987: quoted material.

—Interview with Ralph Watts: quoted material.

—Interview with Walter Williamson: quoted material.

—Eddie Stone, *Donald Writes No More* (Los Angeles: Holloway House, 1974): quoted material.

—Interview with Bentley Morriss: quoted material.
—Interview with Paul Lee: quoted material.
—Interview with Dr. Kenneth Cole: quoted material.
—La Liberte' de l'Est: quoted material.
—Interview with Robert Skinner: quoted material.